Law and Society

With Procedural, Criminal and International law

Law and Society

With Procedural, Criminal and International law

"From the perspective of a country, Sweden, with a long tradition of democracy and human rights and with a comparison to a country in the former Soviet Union, Belarus."

C-G Ekström

Dan Ogvall

Copyright appendix 2, about Belarus: Zhanna Kanavalava

Translation from Swedish: Darya Sukhorukova

Legal English Editor: Mace Simon

Contact publisher: e-mail cege.ekstrom@mailbox.swipnet.se

ISBN 978-1-105-91919-0

Preface

Law and society treats law and the legal process viewed from both a societal and the individual's point of view, from the perspective of a small European country, Sweden. The material has a strong sense of reality with the knowledge necessary to understand the legal system. The book includes six chapters dealing separately with different parts of the legal system. The last chapter treats European and international common law

The text explains legal terms and conditions in everyday English. In connection with the text are brief summary reports of actual court cases to provide increased practical understanding. Short extracts from the statutory text is interspersed to provide a direct link to the legal concepts and context described in the book. At the end of each chapter there are checkpoints with short questions. In some chapters there are stories with portraits of a professional role within the legal field.

In two appendixes there is a comparison between the legal system in Sweden and in a developing country in the former Soviet Union, Belarus.

Authors and partners

C-G Ekström: Social scientist, college teacher and author of textbooks, Goteborg, Sweden

Dan Ogvall : Former judge of a district court, mediator and arbitrator, Goteborg, Sweden

Zhanna Kanavalava: PhD in law, teacher at Belarusian Trade and Economics University of Consumer Cooperatives, Gomel, Belarus (responsible for appendix 2)

Darya Sukhorukova: Translator, Minsk, Belarus

Mace Simon: Attorney at law, California, USA and educator, Goteborg, Sweden

Contents

1. Legal system 1

2. Judicial System 19

3. Procedural Law - Disputes.. 45

4. Procedural Law – Criminal Cases 61

5. Criminal Law 73

6. International Law.. 95

Appendix 1: Comparison of the legal system in Sweden and in
Belarus... 115

Appendix 2: Foundations of the Constitutional System of the
Republic of Belarus... 119

1

The legal system

A developed country needs a legal system in order to function. Citizens must have confidence that the country's laws and regulations are enforced. It can be said that a state's aim should be a democratically determined legislation that is applied to everyone. Since Sweden is a member of the EU, the EU's legal system is of great importance in our country.

Legislation

Legal Rules

The system of legal rules is known as the *legal system*. This system is not set in stone but can be changed with the change of views in society, or when the governing politicians want to change people's attitudes. For example, in recent years, the perception of gender equality and attitude towards women has been affected among other things by the mass media coverage. This can then lead to changes in legislation or sometimes to introduction of entirely new laws.

    Laws are established by the state and are available in written form, so that all the citizens can be aware of them and can keep to them. It is the Swedish Parliament (Riksdag) that establishes (decides on) laws. Draft laws are issued either by the government in the form of government bills or by individual members of the Parliament in the form of bills. This can give source to further studies. It is the Ministry of Justice, which is the part of the Government Administration, that is responsible for legislation and courts. On the government's website www.regeringen.se you can find information on government policies, study proposals as well as government bills, etc.

The government has the right to issue so-called decrees - more detailed rules regarding a law. Laws and decrees can be called with one term - statutes. Both statutes and decrees are published in the Swedish Code of Statutes (SFS) and are also available on www.riksdagen.se, www.lagrummet.se and www.notisum.se.

In addition to the statutes, the authorities have the right to decide on practical rules and instructions, so-called regulations, which affect their areas of work. Such regulations can be found on a relevant authority's website. In some cases, these authority's regulations are also called statutes such as the Code of the Work Environment Statutes (AFS).

By administrative authority is meant municipal and state activities that function on the basis of political decisions, i.e. decisions made by the government, municipality, regional board and other bodies, such as ministries (state) and councils (municipality).

Laws, decrees and administrative rules are usually collectively referred to as *legal rules*:

- Statutes (laws) - adopted by the Swedish Parliament
- Decrees - adopted by the Government
- Administrative Rules - adopted by a relative body

Some Legal Basic Concepts

Legal rules can be divided into two key areas:

- Civil law – concerns relationship among individuals and businesses
- Public law - concerns relationship between authorities on the one hand and private individuals and companies on the other.

In civil matters there are

- Mandatory rules that provide "minimum-protection" of a weaker party
- Optional rules that can be changed by agreement

Those who are affected by legal rules can be

- Physical individuals (persons)
- Legal entities (e.g. corporation, association and authority)\

Bills

A bill can be introduced when a person or several people propose an *initiative* to a change of any kind. The initiative can concern a new law or a change of an existing law. A bill can be proposed by a member of Parliament by submitting a suggestion (*motion*) to the Parliament, whereafter the government appoints a state *investigation committee*. The cause of a motion can be, for example, a proposal from the general public or from organizations and associations. Government can also take the initiative to start an investigation. The investigation committee usually consists of experts in the area and politicians.

The investigation committee delivers the analysis and suggestions in the form of a *report* to the government, the so-called SOU-report (Swedish Government Official Reports, www.sou.gov.se). SOU is numerated as a publishing series for each year, for example, SOU 2011:34. The investigative work can be a rather long-time process, so there is an alternative way to get a bill. If it is a particularly urgent issue, the government can draw up a *ministry memorandum* in order to adopt a law faster. In both cases, it is a ministry, for example the Minister of Agriculture, that is responsible for the bill to be *submitted for comments* before the government formulates the final draft. The report or bill goes through the so-called consultation in order to get the opinions of relevant bodies and organizations. The latter can be trade unions, interest groups or associations that can express their views on the bill and submit them to the Ministry.

Submission for comments of a bill is an old tradition in Sweden. The comments made in the statement of opinion provide excellent opportunities for the creation of well-grounded bills. The government considers all the different opinions that can sometimes be contradictory.

After studying the statement of opinions, the government prepares a *draft* (bill) which is first submitted to the *Council on Legislation* for comments. The Council consists primarily of judges from the Supreme Court and the Supreme Administrative Court (see Chapter 2). The Council on Legislation first examines the bill and checks if it is consistent with other laws and if all of the bill's regulations are coherent. When the government considers the assessment of the Council on Legislation it can make a choice, whether or not to pass the bill or to hand it over to the Parliament, probably after corrections.

One or more *committees* of the Parliament, such as the Agriculture Committee, are referred the bill for consideration. After consideration by the committee, the government writes a final report which is discussed in the Parliament. After that goes the voting, and if the majority of the MPs vote for (approve) the bill, it becomes a statute or law. The Parliament reports the decision to the government which then issues (promulgates) the law that is subsequently published in *the Swedish Code of Statutes (SFS)*.

Example

Since the beginning of the 2000s, requests for smoking bans in restaurants have been reported. The issue has also been included in the bills to the Parliament. The government (Ministry of Health and Social Affairs) submitted the comments of the Council on Legislation in early November 2001. It was not until late 2003 when the bill on a smoking ban was finalized. It was supported by three parliamentary parties that had the majority in the Parliament. The new law (SFS 2004:585) was introduced as a part of the Tobacco Act (SFS 1993:581) and came into effect on January 1, 2005 and also covered other public places in addition to restaurants.

Restrictions on smoking in some indoor premises and outdoor areas

2 §. Smoking is prohibited

(1) on premises intended for childcare, school-related activities, or other activities for children and young people, as well as on school playgrounds and similar areas at pre-schools and after-school recreation centres,

(2) on premises intended for healthcare and medical treatment,

(3) in areas of residential facilities that are intended for joint use, and at facilities offering special services or care,

(4) on domestic public transport facilities, and on premises intended for the use of those travelling by such facilities,

(5) in restaurants and other facilities where food and drink are served, with the exception of outdoor service areas,

(6) in other facilities and in the settings specified in subsections 1-5; when a public gathering or event of the type specified in part 2, sections 1-3 of the Public Order Act (1993:1617) is arranged; in facilities intended for use by participants in connection with public gatherings or events; and

(7) in other facilities of the types specified in subsections 1-6 and to which the general public have access.

Swedish Code of Statutes (SFS)

Laws and decrees are regularly published as they are adopted by the Parliament. They are published in the Swedish Code of Statutes (SFS) and are available on www.riksdagen.se, www.lagrummet.se or www.notisum.se. You can search by a keyword, official title of the law or SFS number that consists of the year and a serial number, for example, 2010:570.

Keywords
Title
Number, e.g. 2010:570

If a law is changed by the Parliament the new law can either get a new SFS code (re-published) or it can be changed under the "Act amending the Act

..." For example, the SFS 2010:570 Act amending the Act (2007:1091) on Public Procurement. The Act on Public Procurement will retain its SFS 2007:1091 number but the text is updated according to SFS 2010:570. There is then an entry in the new text by which the SFS code is changed.

Legislative work

- Study proposal (or ministry memorandum) is submitted to the government
- Possibility for administrative bodies, organizations, etc. to submit their comments
- The Council on Legislation (Supreme Court lawyers) gives its opinion (referral to the Council on Legislation) to the relevant parliamentary committee on the bill's layout and on whether the bill is consistent with other laws
- The government elaborates the bill that is submitted to the Parliament
- Parliamentary Committee submits its report to the Parliament
- The Parliament makes a decision (adopts or rejects)
- If the bill is adopted, the government issues a law which is published in the SFS

The Constitution

The Constitution is the *Instrument of Government* (which specifies how the country is governed), the *Order of Succession* (rules on the royal power), the *Fundamental Law on Freedom of Expression* and the *Freedom of the Press Act*. The Constitution is so important for democracy that it can only be changed by two Parliament resolutions and by the Parliament's voting.

Fundamentals of the State Form of Government

The fundamental rules of the Swedish state form of government, such as freedom of opinion, freedom of assembly, respect for human dignity and the country's form of government are in the first chapter of the Instrument of Government.

It also indicates that the Parliament is the people's foremost representative which among other things legislates and decides on the state's budget and taxes. The King or the Queen, according to the order of succession, is the official head of state, but in practice it is the government that rules the country. The government is accountable to the Parliament. Sweden's municipalities and county councils are governed by local elected councils that may charge taxes on the citizens.

Forms of Government in Other Countries

In other countries the division between the Head of State and the government can differ from that in Sweden. In those European countries that have a *monarchy*, i.e. king or queen, the monarchs no longer have a direct power. The king or the queen has instead a so-called representative role as the country's representative during various events and visits. In other countries, the king or the queen has more power, e.g. in Saudi Arabia and Jordan.

Countries that have a *republic* as a form of government usually have a *president* as head of state. A president can either have a representative role or a greater political power. In France and the Czech Republic, for example, the president has more power than the president in Germany and in several other EU countries. Outside the EU, the president can often have a greater power, e.g. in the U.S. and Brazil. Common to most democratic countries in the world is that the basic political power is held by parliament elected by popular vote which usually also appoints the government. The head of government (Prime Minister) thus has a significant influence on the country's politics. In countries with a strong presidential power, the president nominates and appoints government officials, shares political power with the parliament, and prepares the national budget.

The 27 EU member states, including Sweden, have handed over a part of political power, including legislation, to the EU Commission and the EU Parliament. Most EU regulations must be first adopted by the Swedish Parliament before they are applied. The same applies to the members of the European Commission on Human Rights, including Sweden. Even the United Nations' (UN) members have to abide by certain rules (conventions) in their legislation, such as the Convention on the Rights of the Child.

Freedom of Expression

An important part of the Swedish democratic government is that everyone can freely express their views in various ways without hindrance or censorship. If an expressed opinion is contrary to any law, for example, it implies that a person or a group of persons is defamed or subjected to persecution, the suspect can be prosecuted in court for the crime (see Chapters 4-5). No authority may prevent a person from self-expression in a certain way even if it is considered to be criminal.

Freedom of the Press

Freedom of the press according to the Freedom of the Press Act means the right to freely express one's views in writing. Freedom of press also means freedom to post pictures, but not to defame other people or make them feel abused. The Press Ombudsman (PO) deals with complaints from people who consider themselves abused by the press (www.po.se). Further, one must not "endanger state security" in writing, for example by revealing military secrets.

Public Record

The Freedom of the Press Act also regulates several other key democratic rights, e.g. the public has a right to access and read the so-called *public documents* of the municipal and state authorities. This right also gives newspapers, radio and television the opportunity to monitor and study documents regarding official decisions, accountancy, etc. This *principle of public access to official records* is unique for the Scandinavian countries and it is not subsumed in other countries, even within the EU. However, there are certain limitations to the principle of publicity such as documents referring to national security, personal information and information regarding the control of crime. These restrictions on freedom of information are more fully discussed in the Publicity and Secrecy Act of 2009.

Right to Anonymity

Another important democratic right is that the authorities may not try to find out where, for example, a journalist got his information in order to try to influence or even threaten a journalist's source of information.

The Statute Book

The laws can be divided into three types: *fundamental (constitutional) laws, codes* and other laws (Appendix). Such division is also used in the oldest statute books: Norstedts, The Law Book (Swedish: Sveriges Rikes Lag, Norstedts). The second statute book is Swedish Laws, Thomson Fakta (Swedish: Thomson Fakta Sveriges Lagar) which has instead a division in legal areas, e.g. national law, family law, housing law, etc. Both the statute books are referring to so-called precedents in the sections of laws. Please note that the statute books are not issued by the state, but by private publishers.

Laws and regulations are also available on the Internet, e.g. on the Parliament's website (see above) and the Swedish Body of Laws SL available on www.notisum.se.

The Codes

As mentioned above, besides the fundamental laws there are also codes. They include the fundamental rules within the legal framework. The division into codes in the statute book follows the law of 1734, and that is why the name (Swedish: balk) is rather old-fashioned. The contents have of course changed since then, but the archaic language is still sometimes apparent. Here are several of the codes:

- Marriage Code
- Children and Parents Code
- Inheritance Code
- Code of Land Laws, the Real Property Code
- Construction Code
- Commercial Code
- Penal Code
- Code of Judicial Procedure
- Execution Code
- Environmental Code

Besides, there are some other important laws placed together with the codes, including the following:

- Registration of Property Law
- Administrative Judicial Procedure Act
- Law of Damages
- Bankruptcy Law

Where are the laws applied?

The Swedish laws apply primarily to what happens in Sweden. In different ways they apply to all people who are in Sweden, irrespective of whether they are residents or are just visiting. The Swedish legislation may also apply to what happens abroad, such as crimes committed by the Swedish residents. Sweden has agreements with other countries concerning the law applicable in certain situations such as divorce.

EU Rules

Sweden, together with 26 other countries is a member of the European Union (EU). Member states must in some areas adapt their legislation to the EU *Directive*. So far, it concerns mostly laws on economic issues, as well as labor, consumerism, environmental and agricultural issues. The aim is to create equal conditions for freedom of movement of goods, services, capital and labor within the EU area. This means that the member states must have similar laws in several legislative areas, known as the *harmonization of laws*.

EU Regulation

Different legislations in all EU countries would be an obstacle for the freedom of movement. The adaptation means that the EU directive must be introduced as a Swedish law. In some cases, the EU decision can be introduced immediately without having to be first introduced in the Swedish law by means of the so-called EU *regulation*. However, some important legal areas are outside of the cooperation, such as criminal law and family law.

EU Directive

As a member of the European Union (EU), Sweden like other EU countries must adapt its laws to the *EU Directive*. It is designed by the EU Council of Ministers, and the European Parliament must give its approval. The Council is composed of ministers from all the EU countries. If, for example, the directive concerns environmental issues, it is the ministers of the governments that form the Council of Ministers. However, it is the EU Commission that ultimately designs the directives.

All EU countries have to follow EU Directives when formulating their own laws, but they can be adapted to the country's situation in a certain way. The EU Commission can also issue the so-called EU *Regulations* that will be binding for the member states, but that do not have to be included in the countries' legislation.

Example

The current Swedish Law on Competition which facilitates and sustains a sound competition between companies has its background in the EU directives. It has been adapted to the Swedish conditions and has thus not exactly the same content as the directives. The spirit of the law is the same in all EU countries: it facilitates trade in the European area.

EU Directive – is adapted to the Swedish law

EU Regulation – is applied as a Swedish law

European Convention

The European Convention that is commonly known as the European Convention for the Protection of Human Rights and Fundamental Freedoms was adopted in 1950. The Convention includes the right to liberty and personal security, right to fair trial, right to respect of private and family life, freedom of thought, conscience and religion, freedom of speech, freedom of association and the right of assembly, and a ban on discrimination.

European Convention is exercised by the Council of Europe which today comprises 47 member countries, including Sweden. Most European countries are members of the Council of Europe, including Russia and Ukraine, but there is an exception: Belarus.

The Council of Europe

The Council of Europe makes regular assessments of how the states execute their commitments in various fields as the members of the Council of Europe. These commitments are based largely on the European Convention on Human Rights, but also on other European conventions in the legal, social and cultural fields.

Judicial monitoring is done by the European Court of Human Rights. Since its creation the Court has passed 9,000 judgments. Additionally, a large number of complaints are settled by the decisions of the Court.

Sweden follows the European Convention according to § 23, Chapter 2 of the Constitution, but despite it Sweden has had several judgments against it in the European Court.

- - - - - - - - - - - -

§ **23** Act or other provision may not be in contravention of Sweden's commitments under the European Convention for the Protection of Human Rights and Fundamental Freedoms. Law (1994:1468).

- - - - - - - - - - - -

Legal Case

<u>The European Court's Judgment of case (2008-12-16) of Khurshid
Mustafa et al against Sweden</u>

Summary: The background of the complaint was briefly as follows. A
married couple lived together with their children in a rented apartment
in Stockholm. The lease was terminated by the landlord in April 2004
because the appellants had installed and then did not implement a
dismantling of a satellite dish in accordance with the landlord's
request.

In the final decision the Court of Appeal found that the appellants
failed to fulfill their obligations with regard to the installation of the
satellite dish, and so the lease would not be extended. The court further
determined that the family would be granted a three-month suspension
before they would have to leave the apartment. Thereafter, the landlord
offered the appellants the opportunity to stay in the apartment provided
they remove the satellite dish. However, the appellants moved to a new
home.

The appellants claimed before the court that their right to receive
information under Article 10 of the Convention was violated, that their
right to privacy and home under Article 8 was not respected, and that is
why they had to move from their home. The European Court found that
the complaint fell within Article 10 and the Court of Appeal's decision
that the lease should be terminated because the appellants had not
dismantled the satellite dish was an "interference" of their right under
Article 10 – the article's second paragraph. In order to be compatible
with the Convention, such an interference requires support of the law,
that it serves a legitimate purpose and that it is necessary in a
democratic society in relation to the stated purposes. The court found
that the interference satisfied the first two criteria.

The Court found that the third criterion was not met because the
court of appeal had not executed a reasonable proportionality weighing.
The court therefore held that the eviction of the appellants was not
"necessary in a democratic society" and that Sweden had thus not
fulfilled its positive obligation to protect the people's right to
information under Article 10. Taking this assessment into
consideration, the court found no need to examine the complaint under
Article 8. The appellants were granted a certain financial compensation

for the additional costs for travel to and from work that were caused by their move, non-material damages of EUR 5,000 and compensation of legal costs. The verdict was unanimous.

Other Legal Sources

If legal provisions do not provide a court with adequate guidance in order to settle a case, other sources of law are used:

- Adjudication (legal case) made by the higher court instances, also known as precedent
- Legislative History
    - Bill (including the Council on Legislation's opinion)
    - Committee Report
    - Study Proposal
- Doctrine, i.e. literature on jurisdiction
- Other so-called norms formation
    - Agreements (including so-called standard agreements)
    - Custom, trade custom, professional practices, etc
    - Self-regulation, e.g. by codes of conduct (ethics) and professional committees
- Analogy interpretation, i.e. laws close in meaning that do not directly relate to the area concerned, are used in the absence of applicable legislation.

Where can we find the sources of law?

- Statutes (SFS) can be found both on **www.riksdagen.se** and **www.notisum.se,** or you can search for an act name in the indefinite form in Google.
- Legal cases can be found on www.rattsinfosok.dom.se or in the New Legal Archive (NJA) that can be accessed via subscription to Norstedts Law or Thomson Reuters.
- Committee reports are available on www.riksdagen.se, and study proposals - on www.regeringen.se.

- Government Official Reports – SOU – are available on www.sou.gov.se
- Doctrine is literature that can be borrowed from libraries or purchased in bookstores (search via Google).
- Other ways of norm formation can be searched via Google.

Norms vs. Social Rules

Rules of law are norms that are to be followed while social rules are rules of courtesy and decencies. Although the latter are optional, they can facilitate communication between people. Moral codes are in the gray area and they are stronger than social rules but do not always have to be followed. Examples of moral codes can be infidelity which is not prohibited by Swedish law or lying which in some cases may be prohibited, e.g. false testimony in court, but in other cases it is not a crime. Moral codes can become so strong that they can eventually give rise to rules of law.

A Little Bit of History of Law

The modern jurisprudence can be said to have arisen through the so-called Roman law. The Roman Republic created "the Twelve Tables" in year 449 BC, partly to protect the lower class (plebeians) against abuse from the upper class (patricians), and to assure the impartial and consistent application of law. The Roman law developed through legislation, court cases and with the help of legal scholars (legal consultants). The law eventually became opaque and was summarized in a sort of a book of law (Corpus Juris Civilis). The Roman law was studied at European universities since the Middle Ages and was also important for the Church's legal framework (canon law), particularly in family law.

In the Middle Ages commercial life flourished primarily in the major medieval trading cities, especially in Venice and Verona in Italy and Hanseatic cities of Northern Europe: Hamburg and Visby. The trading practices and customs that had been developed there became the basis for many of today's civil laws (lex mercatoria, in Latin).

Since the late 1700s, as nation states grew in importance, it became increasingly imperative for every country to have more congregated laws. Napoleon's body of laws - Civil Code ("Code Napoleon") - became of great significance in many countries in Central and Southern Europe. In Northern Europe the German law book - Bürgerliches Gesetzbuch (BGB) - became of great importance and has influenced the current legislation in Sweden and other countries.

In Sweden the national legislation developed later than in Central and Southern Europe. The Swedish legal system came first through the so-called provincial laws that were created in 1200s- 1300s, at the beginning consisting mostly as memo notes. Around 1350 King Magnus Eriksson gathered all the laws in a general state law and a general city law. At the same time he modernized the laws. Later they were revised and published as Kristoffer's general state law that was supplemented with court practice. We can say that this state law is the basis of the book of law of 1734 that contains the codes system that still exist in the Swedish legal system, though in general the content has been changed and expanded.

Checkpoint Chapter 1

Explain briefly what is meant by:

A. Legal system

B. Bill

C. Investigation Committee

D. Report to the government

E. Swedish Government Official Reports

F. Submission for comments

G. Council on Legislation

H. Legal Rule

I. Law

J. Legal decree

K. The Swedish Code of Statutes

L. Constitution

M. Legislative history
N. Analogy Interpretation
O. Doctrine
P. Custom
Q. Adjudicative Precedent
R. European Convention
S. Social rule
T. Moral rule
U. Roman law
V. Provincial law

2

Judicial System

The judicial system works for the individual's safety and security according to law. When talking about the judicial system we mean Police, Procuratorate, National Board of Forensic Medicine, National Economic Crimes Bureau, Correctional Care, the Swedish Courts (the National Courts Administration) and the National Council for Crime Prevention and Crime Victim Compensation and Support Authority.

The judicial system is also responsible for prevention and investigation of crimes, suing (prosecuting and adjudicating) people, execution of imposed sanctions (punishment), settlement of disputes and protection of the rights of victims. See www.regeringen.se.

Police

The police prevent crime, monitor public order and safety, scout and make criminal investigations. When the police or prosecutors learn that a crime has occurred, it shall be investigated. Police identify what has happened and who may have been involved. The police also consider information they get from the pathologist and forensic scientists. Forensic evidence, such as DNA, can sometimes solve a crime. Police investigators are important in a criminal investigation. They can for instance follow a suspect at a distance in order to get more ideas in the criminal investigation.

Photo: Kristoffer Tessman

If the police obtain information that further strengthens the suspicion, it can be said that the person is suspected on probable cause. A prosecutor may, if the offense is sufficiently serious, ask the district court for a permit to detain a person. If there are sufficient reasons for prosecution, the police conclude its investigation and hand over the case to the prosecutor who takes the case to court. If the police decide to conduct an investigation, they are trying to find out who may be suspected and whether the evidence is sufficient to prosecute.

Criminal investigation is called *preliminary investigation* and is conducted by a prosecutor or a police officer. A preliminary investigation usually begins with the police questioning everyone who can provide information about the suspected offense. The police usually lead the investigation during the investigation phase analyzing who can be suspected of the crime. When the police come so far that someone can be reasonably suspected in a crime, the prosecutor takes over the investigation management. Investigation of less serious crimes as e.g. shoplifting, traffic offenses and theft can usually be continued by police.

When police seize a suspect of a crime they report the fact of detainment to the prosecutor and conduct a questioning of the suspect. After the questioning the prosecutor decides whether the suspect should be *arrested*, i.e. remain in detention, or whether he or she should be *released.* The prosecutor has three days to go to court and request a detention of the suspect in custody; otherwise the suspect will be released.

The Office of the Public Prosecutor

The prosecutor plays an important role in the judicial system - police, prosecutor, court and prison. It is the prosecutor who within the law determines whether prosecution should be instituted or not and appears in court for the state. Prosecution means that the prosecutor requests the court to determine whether a suspect is guilty in a particular crime. The prosecutor also leads the preliminary investigation in many cases.

Decisions on arrest and detention are made by prosecutors under Chapter 24 of the Judicial Code and it is typically required that the suspect is suspected of a crime on a probable cause that can impose a punishment of imprisonment for at least one year. Prosecutor can make decisions of detention if there is a risk that a suspect will be hiding, will continue his criminal activities or will impede the investigation by e.g. removing evidence.

Detention is a deprivation of liberty decided by the district court at the request of the prosecutor. A person who is suspected of a crime *on probable cause* that can lead to imprisonment of at least one year may be detained if there is a risk that he/she may flee the jurisdiction, remove evidence or continue his/her criminal activities. Anyone who is *reasonably suspected* may be detained for further investigation if it is *exceedingly* important. Detention must never happen if it is obvious that the punishment will not exceed a fine. Performance of detention must be made promptly and no later than noon of the third day after the decision of detention was made.

The prosecutor's activities are exercised in the country's 39 public prosecution offices. Everyday crimes, or usual crimes that happen every day, are the major part of prosecutors' work. They include such crimes as theft, shoplifting, assault and damage. At most public prosecution offices there are specialists for environmental crimes, serious violent crimes and drug offenses. Public prosecution offices work in close cooperation with the police who conduct the operational investigations.

ÅKLAGARMYNDIGHETEN

There are three *international public prosecution offices* in the country. They are specialized in organized and transboundary crimes and in international cooperation among prosecutor offices. There are also four *national public prosecution offices* - one anti-corruption office, one that deals with environmental and working environment issues, one - with security and terrorism cases, and one - with criminal charges against police officers.

Swedish National Economic Crimes Bureau

The Swedish National Economic Crimes Bureau is a center for economic crime prevention in Sweden. It investigates accounting violations, bankruptcy-related crimes, tax offence, insider trading and EU-frauds, as well as other complex financial crimes that demand special knowledge in financial conditions and business conditions. The Swedish National Economic Crimes Bureau is primarily focused on serious economic crime, but also on the less serious financial crime in which punishment value is not high, but where the proceedings (prosecution) have a preventive purpose. The Economic Crimes Bureau leads investigation and starts prosecutions where appropriate, in cooperation with the Office of the Public Prosecutor, Police, the Tax Agency, the Financial Supervisory Authority, Customs, trade organizations and industrial companies, etc.

Swedish Prison and Probation Service

The Swedish Prison and Probation Service is a state authority under the government and the Parliament. Those who serve their sentences must do it in a secure way, and it cannot be possible for them to commit crimes during their imprisonment. The preparation for release is a gradual process that starts on the first day of enforcement of the penalty. An important aim of the Prison and Probation Service is to reduce the recidivism rate. It can be achieved through active advocacy, including treatment programs, employment and opportunity for inmates to improve the lack of school attendance. The Swedish Prison and Probation Service employs approximately 9,000 people, most of whom are prison officers. This work is conducted (as per 2010) at 31 detention rooms, 55 penal institutions and 35 probation and parole offices.

Crime Victim Compensation and Support Authority

The Crime Victim Compensation and Support Authority protects victim's rights, interests and needs. If the person who committed a crime cannot compensate the damage and if there is no insurance for the damage, the victim may be entitled to criminal damage compensation from state resources. This right can be used even if the criminal is unknown. The compensation covers primarily personal injuries and violation of integrity.

Victims Fund supports research and other victim-oriented projects driven in nonprofit, public or the private sector. The fund is built up mainly by a special 500 SEK fee which every convicted person is required to pay if the offense is punishable by imprisonment. Annually the fund distributes about 30 million SEK. The Crime Victim Compensation and Support Authority can gather and spread information and research results in order to contribute to a better treatment and support of crime victims.

National Council for Crime Preventing

The National Council for Crime Preventing (BRÅ) is a center for research and development activities in the judicial system. An important starting point for the Swedish criminal policy is to work in order to prevent crime. The National Council for Crime Prevention is an agency that works to reduce crime and increase security in society by producing data and spreading knowledge on crime and crime prevention. The National Council for Crime Prevention also publishes data on the official crime statistics, evaluates reforms, conducts research to generate knowledge and supports local crime prevention work. The National Council for Crime Prevention works on behalf of the Swedish Government and often in collaboration with other agencies and organizations.

Crime Statistics is published annually and provides an overall presentation of the official crime statistics.

National Board of Forensic Medicine

The National Board of Forensic Medicine is an administrative judicial governmental agency. The National Board of Forensic Medicine often deals with finding the cause of death when a person dies unexpectedly or when the police consider that the death was caused by unnatural reasons. In order to get expert help to find out what happened, the police and prosecutors turn to specialists in forensic medicine. In Sweden there are six such departments: in Umeå, Uppsala, Stockholm, Linkoping, Gothenburg and Lund. Every year all the departments get more than 5,000 assignments. There are biomedical scientists, chemists, doctors, psychologists and forensic social investigators working in the National Board of Forensic Medicine. The specialists of the National Board of Forensic Medicine also teach at universities and act on behalf of municipalities, health care and Swedish Prison and Probation Service.

Swedish Courts

To be tried by an impartial and independent court is a fundamental right of every Swedish citizen and every Swedish company. As part of the judicial system, the Swedish Courts' main aim is to ensure an individual's legal security and due process. In the Swedish constitution the courts have an independent status. Neither the Parliament nor any other authority may determine how a court should judge individual cases. The courts' work is governed partly by rules in the Code of Judicial Procedure.

The Swedish courts consist of many different authorities and court committees: the Supreme Court, courts of appeal, district courts, the Supreme Administrative Court, administrative courts of appeal, administrative courts, rent and tenancy tribunals, the Legal Aid Authority and the National Courts Administration.

Swedish courts' main tasks are to settle private disputes, criminal cases, disputes between individuals and government authorities, rent and tenancy disputes as well as to deal with legal aid cases. The courts judge in accordance with the laws that the Parliament adopts.

 # SVERIGES DOMSTOLAR

There are three types of courts in Sweden: *general courts* that consist of district courts, courts of appeal and the Supreme Court; *administrative courts*, i.e. county administrative courts, administrative courts of appeal and the Supreme Administrative Court; and *special courts (tribunals)* that resolve disputes in various specific areas, for example, the Labour Court and the Market Court. See: www.domstol.se.

	General courts	**Administrative courts**	**Special courts**
1st instance	District Courts	Administrative Court	Labour Court Market Court, etc.
2nd instance	Courts of Appeal	Administrative Courts of appeal	
3d instance	The Supreme Court	The Supreme Administrative Court	

District Courts

The district court is the first court of the first instance that deals with criminal and civil cases. The district court also handles other types of cases, such as adoptions, divorces and bankruptcies. There are 49 district courts spread across the country, from Ystad in the south to Gällivare in the north, and they have local support.

Courts of Appeal

If a person is not satisfied with the district court's judgment, he can address the court of appeal in most cases. There are six courts of appeal in the country.

In many cases, however, a review permit must be submitted to the court of appeal in order for a matter to be handled. The court of appeal may, in acquittal of a criminal case, issue the review permit to the prosecutor if the imposed penalty is imprisonment for at most six months or if the district court has made a mistake. The defendant may similarly, for example, get a review permit provided the imposed penalty is higher than a fine or if the district court has made a mistake.

Review permits for both criminal and civil cases shall be granted if

1. there is a reason to doubt the accuracy of the final decision of the district court,

2. it is not possible to estimate the accuracy of the final decision of the district court without such permission,

3. it is important for the conduct of the adjudication process that the appeal is heard by a higher court, or

4. there are other important reasons to consider the appeal.

The Supreme Court

The Supreme Court (HD – from the Swedish "Högsta domstolen") is the final instance for appeals, but not all cases are appealed here. In order to appeal to the Supreme Court a *review permit* is required which is given by the Supreme Court itself. In general, obtaining the review permit applies only to those cases where it is important to obtain a judgment that could play a guiding role for the country's district courts and courts of appeal. Such judgments are called precedents. This means that a district court or a court of appeal, in practice, becomes the final instance in most cases.

Rent Tribunal

In a dispute between a tenant and a landlord, or between a housing cooperative and a house owner the rent tribunal can mediate and in some cases arbitrate the dispute if the parties themselves cannot agree. It can involve disputes over rent, assignments or subleases. The Rent Tribunal also makes decisions on certain issues, such as the right to rent an apartment in second-hand. The Rent Tribunal's decision may be appealed to the Svea Court of Appeal.

Case Example

Rental agreement termination for late payments

Court of Appeal's Decision: Despite 16 late rent payments the rent tribunal concluded that it would be unreasonable to let the rental agreement be terminated. The tribunal took into consideration the tenant's willingness to pay future rent on time and the tenant's personal circumstances: a single parent with three children and engaged in a business activity. It was also taken into consideration that the tenant in good faith relied upon another person to pay the rent, although the landlord had warned that the agreement would be terminated if the delays continued. The Court of Appeal, however, considered that the agreement should be terminated. The delays have continued and now there is a rental debt.

Source www.infotorgjuridik.se

Labour Court

The Labour Court (AD – from the Swedish "Arbetsdomstolen") is a special court that deals with labour disputes. A labour dispute is a dispute concerning the relationship between employers and employees, for example when an employee quits or is fired. The labour court has essentially the same trial procedure as the general courts.

There are two requirements for a labour dispute to be brought directly to the labour court. The action must be commenced by an employer's organization, a trade union or an employer whose employee infringed a collective labour agreement. Additionally, the case has to concern a dispute of a collective agreement, a dispute according to the union participation in decision-making regulated by law or a dispute between the parties or the workplace that are bound by a collective agreement.

For an employee who is not a member of or is not supported by any trade union the action must first be commenced before a district court. The same applies to an employer who is not supported by any employer's organization. If a party is dissatisfied with the district court's decision in a dispute like this, such appeal can be addressed to a labour court. The labour court's judgment is a final decision on a dispute and the judgment may not be further appealed.

Case Example

The Labour Court: 2002-45

The issue to be decided was whether a municipality had objective cause to dismiss an assistant administrator who allegedly had cooperation problems and handled the assistance cases wrongly. The labour court found that the dismissal was not based on objective reasons because the municipality has not fulfilled its transfer obligations.

Market Court

The Market Court settles issues of competition and marketing. The court handles cases involving free competition and inappropriate (ineligible) marketing. It's the Swedish Competition Authority and the Consumer Ombudsman (KO) who report to the courts. Even companies affected by competitors' behavior can address the courts.

Case Example

The Market Court: 2009:18

A telecommunications company has used the term "mobile broadband" in the marketing company of telephone services and claimed that the service is "the Sweden's best mobile broadband". Since there was no accepted definition of mobile broadband, it was not considered to be at variance with the Marketing Practices Act. However, the company has not been able to demonstrate that its service is "the Sweden's best mobile broadband", and therefore the statement was found misleading and inappropriate. The prohibition was reported to the companies using this statement or other statements with essentially similar meaning.

Administrative Courts

Administrative Court

The Administrative Court (formerly the County Administrative Court) deals with cases on disputes between individuals and companies on the one side and authorities on the other. Examples include taxes, driving license, migration matters or disputes with the insurance office, municipality or the social services committee. The administrative court also decides on apprehension of children, young people or drug addicts, as well as Migration Board's decisions on residence permits or refusals. There are 12 administrative courts in the country, one in each municipality.

Administrative Court of Appeal

Decisions by the administrative court can in some cases be appealed to the administrative court of appeal. A review permit is required for a case to be taken up by the administrative court of appeal. The permit is granted if there is a reason to change the court's decision or if the decision of the court may be of importance as a precedent. In tax cases and cases concerning the care of young people, drug addicts and mentally ill people a review permit is not required. There are four administrative courts of appeal in Sweden – in Gothenburg, Jönköping, Stockholm and Sundsvall.

Supreme Administrative Court

The Supreme Administrative Court in Stockholm is the highest general administrative court and it hears decisions appealed after any of the country's four administrative courts of appeal. The most important task of the Supreme Administrative Court is to provide guidance to courts and others who work with adjudication. In order to appeal to the Supreme Administrative Court, a review permit is required and it is granted only if the Supreme Administrative Court's decision provides guidance on how to assess other similar cases, so-called precedent.

Case Example

The Supreme Administrative Court: 4671-08

The right to transportation service has been approved for (I) an 85-year-old woman who walked with a walker and was suffering from angina, etc., and (II) a 79-year-old woman who walked with a walker outdoors, and was suffering from severe back pain.

Courts in Europe

The EU Court of Justice can settle disputes among the 27 member states of the EU. The EU Court is located in Luxembourg. The court's primary task is to ensure that EU countries' common regulatory framework (EU law) is interpreted and applied uniformly in all member states. Since many legal rules are written in a way that gives possibilities for different interpretations, the EU Court's decisions are important to show member states how the rules should be applied.

The European Court in Strasbourg is the part of the Council of Europe that has 47 member states. The court can consider complaints from individuals who believe that the state does not follow the European Convention for the Protection of Human Rights and Fundamental Freedoms.

Modern Judicial Proceedings

On November 1, 2008, a reform was introduced in the general courts throughout the country. Significant changes were introduced to the Code of Judicial Procedure, i.e. the regulations that govern the legal process in general courts. The general courts are, as mentioned above, district courts, courts of appeal and the Supreme Court.

All hearings in the district court should also be documented with video. The aim is to give the court of appeal a better basis than before in cases appealed. Only hearings have to be recorded on video, not the entire trial. Video recordings will as a rule constitute the oral evidence for the court of appeal when there is an appeal.

An advantage of video documentation is that one usually does not have to come to court more than once to give evidence. Another advantage is that the court of appeal's judgment is based on the same facts as the district court's judgment. However, under the Code of Judicial Procedure it's possible to provide additional evidence in the court of appeal if it is important for the investigation. The defendants in criminal cases should normally be present at the trial in the court of appeal as well as the parties of civil cases.

The sound recording is public, while the image is secret and should not be disclosed to anyone outside the courts. The audience can be recorded on video if they sit directly behind someone who is being interrogated. When the final decision on a case is taken, the video is destroyed.

The district court documents all interviews with video. However, only the hearing, not the entire trial, is recorded.
Source: Swedish courts
Photo: Patrik Svedberg

Verdict

The court's decision is formulated as a verdict (judicial decision). A verdict has to be performed in writing and has to include time and place, parties, attorneys, their claims and objections, the facts they are based on and the grounds for the judgment of what is proven in the case. A verdict by a higher court must, to the extent necessary, include a review of a lower court's verdict. If a party has a right to appeal it must be mentioned in the verdict.

An important principle is that the court in its verdict judges by the so-called the *principle of immediacy, for example, in civil proceedings* under the Code of Judicial Proceedings, Chapter 17 § 2-3. This means that the verdict can be based only on what the parties have referred to during the trial. Similar rules are contained in Chapter 30 of the Code of Judicial Procedure regarding *criminal cases*.

What the verdict should contain can be found in Chapter 17, § 6-7. Mainly the verdict must include the *judgment* itself, i.e., the court's decision, the parties' claims and objections and the *grounds for the decision* which is an explanatory statement for the verdict. The findings must be written in the reverse order, i.e. the judgment comes first and the grounds and justification come after it. In a judgment by default the verdict is written in a simplified form according to Chapter 17, § 8.

If a verdict is appealed, the verdict in higher instance shall include a report on the contents of the verdict of the lower court according to Chapter 17, § 6.

Judge

A judge's task is to assess and settle (judge) different types of judiciary cases. A judge is not a title but a function in a court. The legally qualified judges (educated lawyers) who work at courts can have many different titles.

Young judges may have the title of notary, fiscal or assistant judge. Notaries are lawyers who passed examination after training at a court in order to have the experience beyond the academic studies. During the latter part of the service the notary may under his own responsibility handle some selected types of cases. This service includes some theoretical training. Those who want to go further in their judicial education receive the title of fiscal or assistant judge and then work as judges.

Not only educated lawyers judge in courts, but also lay judges. They are the public representatives in the courts. They are not educated as lawyers, but have completely different professions. The lay judges do not work in court, but get there when required by a trial. They are people appointed by political parties who complement the judge's legal knowledge with different experiences. It is important that the lay judges reflect the Swedish society – the young and the old, men and women, of Swedish or foreign origin. Lay judges are involved primarily in criminal cases, not in civil cases. For example, in the main hearing of a criminal case at a district court, the court is usually composed of one judge and three lay judges.

What does a lay judge do?

The lay judge participates in the judicial activity. The process and the work may seem different depending on whether we are talking about cases in a general court or cases in an administrative court. In general, however, it means that the lay judge is called to the hearing or sitting with a submission by the court. The lay judge is present at the hearing and the subsequent deliberations. Just like the ordinary judge the lay judge is obliged to follow the law in his judicial function. The lay judge also has a right to ask additional questions during the report and hearing. Possible decisions are discussed and positions for or against

---

are expressed after a hearing. Usually the discussion leads to agreement on the outcome. If different opinions are expressed during the deliberations a voting is conducted and the lay judge's vote has the same weight as the ordinary judge's.

Source: www.dom.se

Photo: Lars Lydig

A Profession that Is as Exciting as Important

The thought of becoming a judge appeared while serving as a notary clerk, but Niklas Ljunggren wanted to have more experience first. He had been working at the Ministry of Justice for six years before he in August began his career as a judge at Malmö District Court.

A judge who works at a court can have many different titles, but irrespective of the title the mission is the same: to resolve disputes and to judge matters of various types of cases. As a judge Niklas is one of the four judges present at a hearing. He is a presiding judge and the only judge educated as a lawyer. He judges together with three lay judges. The legally educated judge is responsible for explaining to the lay judges which laws refer to the type of cases they are considering.

- My task is to explain the background for the assessment and what rules are applied in this case. I'm not allowed to control too much, everyone should make their own assessment. What concerns parties' or witnesses' trustworthiness the lay judges have as much life experience and good qualification to make the assessment as a lawyer.

35

Diverse and Unpredictable Days

Niklas describes the work at the district court as diverse and independent. On the days when he sits in the court he organizes his work himself, and contacts with the public make the work unpredictable and very exciting.

- The days at the court are the most diverse days, and perhaps the most stimulating. You meet many new people and you never know in advance how the day will develop.

Being a judge, one faces many types of challenges.

- I contact people who are in crisis situations in life, who are both sad and angry but still must feel that they are well treated and get a real trial. Besides, all the time I have new cases and matters I must put myself in. Once I have judged a case I must leave it behind myself and direct all my concentration to the next one. This requires my readiness to listen and focus on what is presented to me.

Important to be humane

Niklas says that in order to make a process easier for those involved it is important for judges to be humane in their treatment.

- Above all, it matters what happens before judgment – a judge should show that he really listens to what people say and everyone should feel that they have had a chance to present their arguments. I imagine that it is easier to accept a judgment - even if you think that is wrong - if you know that the court has listened to what you have said.

Source: www.dom.se

Photo: Lars Lydig

Legal Assistance

Most people hire an attorney to help them in court, either a lawyer (a member of the Bar Association) or another jurist. A person suspected of a crime may be entitled to a lawyer, a *public defender*, whose work is paid, in whole or in part, by the state. A person is entitled to a public defender if necessary with regard to the investigation of the crime, if a person risks penalties other than fines or probation, or if there are special circumstances of the case or personal circumstances. The court makes decisions whether a public defender is needed. At the trial the court determines which part of the costs for public defender the suspect must pay himself.

Case Example

Svea Court of Appeal Ö9500-8

Application to appoint an attorney located outside the jurisdiction of the court as a public defender was denied because of the increased cost that would create.

Advokaten

In civil cases one can get *legal aid* from the state which starts with a one-hour consultation of a lawyer or other jurist. It is the hired attorney or lawyer who seeks legal aid for the client. Legal aid means that you can get help having to pay a part of the costs in cases that cannot be completed during the consultation period, usually one hour. Legal aid also covers a part of the costs of a person's representative (lawyer). Legal aid may cover up to 100 hours of attorney's work.

Legal aid is given only to individuals, not to associations, companies and similar entities. Estates can in some cases get legal aid. One may not have gross income exceeding 260,000 SEK per year. One should have the need for legal representation and its costs must be reasonable for the state to contribute to it. As a rule one does not get legal aid if the matter concerns a value less than half of the base amount (one base amount was 44,500 SEK in 2013).

If an individual enters into a legal dispute and needs financial help, he or she should primarily use his home or comprehensive household insurance to pay for the *legal protection*. Those who have insurance for *legal protection* cannot usually get legal aid. Legal aid is not provided for those who have no insurance at all, but as a rule everyone has one.

Legal protection is a financial protection that applies if one enters into a legal dispute that can be tried in court. The insurance covers most matters one can enter into as a private individual and compensates the costs for attorney and litigation. Some types of disputes are excluded from the legal protection, such as divorce matters and disputes related to the exercise of the profession. The compensation is usually limited to three base amounts (ca 130,000 SEK) and 20% of the costs are deductible, usually a minimum amount of about 1,500 SEK.

Legal Investigation

Both defence attorneys and prosecutors must make a comprehensive legal analysis to assess whether a case is worth taking to court. The analysis can be schematically described in the following order.

Dispositive facts ---Legal Rule --- Evidence --- Legal consequence

---

It is about performing a so-called legal investigation in the form of laws, cases, preparational statements, practices and doctrine - that will help to win the case. The following parts can be included in a legal investigation:

Dispositive Facts

- The background and circumstances (matter)
- People affected (parties in civil cases, defendants and plaintiffs in criminal cases)
- Process framework, i.e. what the process will be focused on

Legal Rule

- Is there an applicable legal rule?
- Precedent - strong or weak?
- What does the legislative history say?
- What does the doctrine say?
- Other norm settings

Evidence

- Facts that support argumentation

Legal Consequence

- Possible consequence of the above, i.e. the outcome in court

Disqualification

Disqualification is a situation when a decision-maker can be considered biased. The person subject to disqualification is called *challengeable*. This procedure is necessary in order to counteract bias and prejudice. It is required to prevent issues that do not belong in a legal matter to be able to determine the outcome, and to prevent the arousal of suspicion that a decision is not made on objective grounds.

An attorney cannot have a conflict of interest in a case. Challenge (disqualification) may for example occur if an attorney previously supported the opponent in another case or if a colleague at the law firm represents the opposing party. Even a judge or prosecutor may be challengeable, for example, if they are somehow linked to any of the parties, for example in private relationships.

Parliamentary Control

The Parliament is the highest decision-making political body in Sweden, but it is the government that has the operational (running) responsibility to assure that the Parliament's decisions are correct. There are functions of control in the legal system that allow the members of Parliament and the Swedish people to have confidence that the government and the ministers follow the Parliamentary decisions. These functions are referred to as the Parliamentary control according to Chapter 13 of the Constitution (SFS 1974:152), i.e. control of the political power. The following functions can be said to be included into the parliamentary control:

The Parliamentary Committee on the Constitution

The Parliamentary Committee on the Constitution is a parliamentary committee that investigates and makes proposals on major issues concerning the constitution and administration, and examines the work of the Council of State and the government. The Parliamentary Committee on the Constitution has an important function of examination under Chapter 13 Article 1 of the Instrument of Government.

Art. 1. The Committee on the Constitution shall examine ministers' performance of their official duties and the handling of Government business. The Committee is entitled for this purpose to have access to the records of decisions taken in Government matters and to all documents pertaining to such matters. Another Riksdag committee or a member of the Riksdag is entitled to raise in writing with the Committee on the Constitution any issue relating to a minister's performance of his official duties or the handling of Government business. Act (2010:1408).

Art. 2. It shall be incumbent upon the Committee on the Constitution to communicate to the Riksdag, whenever reasons so warrant but at least once a year, any observations it may find worthy of attention in connection with its examination. The Riksdag may make a formal statement to the Government in consequence thereof. Act (2010:1408).

The Parliamentary Ombudsmen

The Parlamentary Ombudsmen review that the courts and the administrative authorities work according to the laws and regulations in force under Chapter 12, Article 6 of the Instrument of Government. The detailed instructions for the work of the Parlamentary Ombudsmen can be found in the Riksdag Act. See also page 70 in the book.

Parliamentary Ombudsmen

Art. 6. The Riksdag elects one or more Parliamentary Ombudsmen to supervise the *application of laws and other statutes in the public service, under terms of reference drawn up by the Riksdag. An Ombudsman may institute criminal and disciplinary proceedings in the cases indicated in these terms of reference.*

An Ombudsman is entitled to be present at the deliberations of a court of law or an administrative authority and shall have access to the records and other documents of such an authority. A court of law or an administrative authority and any State or local government official shall provide an Ombudsman with such information and opinions as he may request. A similar obligation is incumbent upon any other person coming under the supervision of the Ombudsman. A public prosecutor shall assist an Ombudsman if so requested.

More detailed rules concerning the ombudsmen can be found in the Riksdag Act and other acts. Act (2010:1408).

The Swedish National Audit Office

The National Audit Office is responsible for auditing financial reports and performance of the state authorities in accordance with Chapter 12, Art. 7-9 of the Instrument of Government. The detailed instructions for the National Audit Office's work can be found in the Riksdag Act.

National Audit Office

Art. 7. The National Audit Office is an authority under the Riksdag whose function is to audit the activities of the State. More detailed rules concerning the National Audit Office are laid down in the Riksdag Act and elsewhere in law. Act (2010:1408).

Art. 8. The National Audit Office is under the direction of three Auditors General, who are elected by the Riksdag. The Riksdag may remove an Auditor General from office only provided the AuditorGeneral no longer fulfils the requirements for the office or has been guilty of gross negligence.

The Auditors General decide independently, having regard to the rules laid down in law, what activities shall be audited. They determine severally and independently how their audit shall be carried out and formulate their own conclusions on the basis of their audit. Act (2010:1408).

Art.9 *Further provisions for the National Audit Office are laid in the Riksdag Act and other legislation. Act (2010:1408).*

The Parliamentary Control by the Government

The government has its own control function of supervision over authorities and courts, the Chancellor of Justice. The Chancellor of Justice also represents the State in courts as a prosecutor in the freedom of press and expression cases and as the government's legal adviser. The Chancellor of Justice's work is regulated by Act (1975:1339) on the Chancellor of Justice's surveillance, and by Decree (1975:1345) containing instructions for the Chancellor of Justice. See also page 57 of the book.

The Office of the Chancellor of Justice is an authority under the government whose main tasks are:

- to supervise other authorities and even courts on behalf of the government
- to represent the state in court
- to decide on claims for damages against the state

- to be the prosecutor in the press libel and freedom of speech cases, and
- to be the government's legal advisor.

The Chancellor of Justice also supervises the legal aid system and the Bar Association's disciplinary activities. It can be said that the Chancellor of Justice (JK) is the state's primary legal representative or the "State's lawyer."

The Chancellor of Justice Ann Skarhed

Development of Independent Courts

There are many countries in the world that do not have autonomous and independent courts. This applies to most countries with widespread corruption: judges are paid to adjudicate in a certain way. It can refer to countries with a dictatorship where the courts, directly or indirectly, are controlled by the people who have power in the country. Such countries require political changes in order to be able to acquire and develop a functioning legal system. Thereafter, the legal system must be rebuilt from its foundation in order to function in a democracy.

International Legal Assistance Consortium (ILAC) is an international organization that fulfils such tasks. It works on behalf of the United Nations and individual states' relief administrations. ILAC builds up a legal system based on western models and provides training for the lawyers who just started their professional activity. The mentioned countries have often operating courts, but they do not work on the basis of the UN Declaration of Human Rights. ILAC has had missions in countries such as East Timor, Kosovo, Bosnia, Cambodia, Rwanda, Haiti, Iraq, Afghanistan, Angola, Sri Lanka and Sudan. ILAC's headquarters is located in Stockholm (www.ilacinternational.org).

Checkpoint Chapter 2

Explain briefly what is meant by:

A. Judicial system
B. Court
C. District Court
D. Verdict
E. To appeal
F. Special Court
G. Labour Court
H. Administrative Court
I. Administrative Law
J. Legal assistance
K. Attorney
L. Disqualification
M. Legal investigation
N. Dispositive facts
O. Legal consequence

3

Procedural Law - Disputes

Sometimes situations arise where someone feels unfairly treated. Citizens and consumers can feel small compared to companies and government agencies. That is why Sweden and other developed countries have a functioning judicial system. It's about having your case heard by the authorities and courts. It can refer to a large number of issues, ranging from dissatisfaction with a product purchased in a store, a dispute between two people, and to government decisions on taxes, fees, contributions, child custody, etc.

Dissatisfaction with Authority's Decision

Authorities make many different decisions and the person affected may feel unfairly treated. Before the decision is made one can have a discussion with the authority and express his opinion. In many cases a person can also request that the authority reconsiders a decision. With regard to decisions on taxes and tax declarations a person has a right to request a review within five years following the year of decision. If the person is still not satisfied, he can appeal to a general administrative court (see Chapter 2).

Example

Supreme Administrative Court: 7228-04

In a case of unemployment allowance, conditions were the following: a person who voluntarily switched from a full-time position to half-time employment with the same employer was not regarded as unemployed.

Certain administrative decisions, mainly municipal, can first be appealed to the *County Administrative Board* which is the state's coordinating agency in each county. Examples include decisions on the disposal of children, building approval, environmental and nature issues, camera surveillance, animal protection, food handling, etc. (see www.lst.se).

Parliamentary Ombudsmen - JO

The Parliamentary Ombudsman (JO) is elected by the Parliament to control compliance of operations performed by authorities and their officials with applicable laws and regulations. Ombudsmen control it by hearing and investigating complaints from the public and by making visits to the authorities and performing other investigations on their own initiative.

Anyone can complain to the Ombudsman, one does not need to be a Swedish citizen or even live in Sweden. The issue of the complaint does not need to refer to himself. One can complain of government agencies (including courts), municipal and county authorities and even of individual officials of these authorities. One cannot complain of the government, the parliament, local politicians or private companies. A complaint to JO should be made in writing by a letter, fax or e-mail or on the special JO form (see www.jo.se). Application can be written in a free form but it should be clearly stated who you are and what you are complaining about.

JO Ombudsman

Dissatisfaction with Products

Consumer Guidance

In most municipalities there are consumer guidance services where the municipality's residents can turn to for advice and information. The aim is to inform and give advice on consumer issues so that people could make the right decision easier. The service is free of charge.

A person can turn to the service, for example

- prior to purchase in order to learn about test results, market summaries, advice
- after purchase in connection with complaints of products and contacts with companies or
- with questions about consumer laws and a consumer's rights and obligations

The service informs also groups of people, e.g. schools, organizations and workplaces, and maintains contact with local and central authorities on consumer issues, including the state Consumer Agency that provides information and assistance on consumer issues.

Consumer adviser, Lars Sundling
Härryda Municipality

National Board for Consumer Complaints

If a consumer has a complaint, he can turn to the National Board for Consumer Complaints (ARN – from the Swedish Allmänna reklamationsnämnden) which is a state administrative authority. The Board functions much like a court and can impartially deal with disputes between consumers and entrepreneurs (manufacturers). The complaint should be made by the consumer himself or herself.

The Board makes recommendations on how disputes should be resolved, for example, the manufacturer must give the consumer a refund. Usually it takes about six months after the complaint until the decision is made by the Board. The examination is free of charge. The Board's aim is to provide an inexpensive, simple, fast and still legally secure alternative to court litigation. The Board is absolutely impartial during such examinations.

ARN

The chairperson is the head of the Board. The Board consists of department chairpersons the number of which is decided by the government and a number of members representing the interests of consumers and manufacturers. The chairman, vice chairman and department chairs must be lawyers with working experience as judges. They are appointed by the government.

The instruction for the Board specifies its tasks. It is said that the Board:

- examines disputes between consumers and manufacturers related to a product, service or other utility that the manufacturer has provided the consumer with (consumer disputes) and provides recommendations on how the dispute should be resolved

- supports the local consumer activity arbitration in consumer disputes through training, advice and information

The Board's decision on consumer disputes cannot be appealed. Under certain special conditions, however, the Board can reconsider the decision in a case.

Case Example

Decision 2003-5534

J bought a GPS package of a company. According to J the package was sold with a condition that he would be provided with a manual in Swedish. The company denied the claim, arguing that it was not clear at the time of purchase that it was crucial for J that there was a manual in Swedish.

The Board made the following judgment.

According to §16 of the Consumer Purchases Act (1990:932) a product – in order not to be regarded as imperfect – should be accompanied by the necessary instructions for its installation, assembly, use, storage and maintenance. According to the legislative history of the Act (bill 1989/90: 89 p. 97) the instructions are usually written in Swedish. Rescission (cancellation) is the most severe sanction if a product is defective and can only be considered if the defect is essential to the buyer (see § 29 of the same act). The issue of defect's essentiality must be assessed from the buyer's point of view (cf. bill. 1989/90: 89 p. 126).

It appears from what the parties stated in the case that at the time of purchase J and the company discussed that J wanted to have a manual in Swedish. In a view of this, the company must have realized that it was important for him to have it. For that reason, and taking into account the requirement in § 16 Consumer Purchases Act, the Board decided that it may be considered part of the agreement that J must have received a manual that was written in Swedish. Since it did not happen, the fault rests with the company according to § 16 Consumer Purchases Act. Since J obviously needed instructions written in Swedish in order to be able to use the product that Board finds the fault significant. There is thus a basis for cancellation of the purchase. J's claim must be approved.

Comment: Cancellation means that the buyer has the right to return goods to the seller and get the money back.

Most Businesses Execute the Board's Decisions

The National Board for Consumer Complaints' decision is not obligatory for the parties. The decisions cannot be enforced with coercion. A decision is compulsory when it is made by a court or by the Swedish Enforcement Authority and concerns an injunction to pay or judicial assistance.

However, the vast majority of manufacturers (companies) perform the Board's decisions. According to the surveys performed by the Board in cases when a consumer is entirely or partially right, an average of nearly 80 percent of manufacturers act in accordance with the Board's decisions.

Performance varies from department to department. Some trade organizations, such as the Swedish Trade Association and the Association for Motor Retail Trades and Repairs have claimed to be accountable for their members' obligations (responsibilities), if they do not perform the decision of the Board.

The National Board for Consumer Complaints cannot settle

- disputes between individuals or between businesses
- disputes relating to health care (including dental)
- disputes relating to legal services
- disputes relating to purchase of property, cooperative apartments or sight-leasehold rights
- tenancy disputes and disputes with housing cooperatives

Application to the Swedish Board for Consumer Complaints

An application to the Board must be made within six months since the trader in whole or in part rejected the consumer's demands. If the trader does not at all respond to the complaint, it is considered that he / she has rejected the claim.

The Board does not adjudicate disputes in which the value of the claim is below a certain amount according to the following value limits for the Board's different departments:

- 500 SEK: matters relating to shoe, textile and general goods segments

- 1,000 SEK: matters relating to electricity, motor, travel, furniture or laundry segments
- 2,000 SEK: matters relating to banking, mortgage, boat, real estate agents or insurance segments

The Board does not adjudicate disputes with traders outside Sweden. If a person has problems with a purchase from any company abroad via internet, e-commerce, there are in some cases possibilities to complain and have a dispute settled. This can be done via the website www.econsumer.gov. This site was created by consumer agencies in 19 member countries, including Sweden, that are members of the International Consumer Protection and Enforcement Network (ICPEN).

Proceed to Court

If a dispute between a seller (company) and a consumer is not resolved with the help of consumer guides or the Swedish Board for Consumer Complaints, the consumer must *sue* the seller in the district court in a civil case (see below). Such a procedure can be expensive for the consumer if the dispute concerns an amount exceeding half of the basic amount. In this case, the one who loses the case must pay his own and the counterparty's attorney expenses. If the amount is smaller (case on smaller amounts) each party pays its expenses regardless of the outcome.

In the case of tenancy disputes, one usually contacts the Rent and Lease Tribunal (see Chapter 1), both for housings and premises. Labour disputes are settled by the Labour Court (see Chapter 1) if an employee is a member of a trade union, otherwise cases are settled by the district court.

The following laws within the civil law can be applied in connection with such disputes:
-    Law of Contract
-    Sale of Goods Act
-    Promissory Note Law
-    Consumer Purchases Act
-    Consumer Services Act

- Consumer Credit Act
- Code of Land Laws (on real estate)
- Tenancy Act (part of the Code of Land Laws)
- Protection of Employment Law
- Marital Code
- Code on Parents and Children

Civil Cases

Many disputes can involve demands for money, interpretation of an agreement or any other financial obligation. Another large group of civil cases is family law cases such as cases of divorce or cases of children's care, housing, visitation and alimony. Unless the parties themselves or with the help of lawyers agree, a party (plaintiff) *sues* the other (defendant) in a court in a *civil case* to get his/her demands to be met.

What type of court will it be?

In civil cases the court which is in charge of a case is determined by the district where the defendant lives (domicile). For those who do not have a known residence the district is determined by their location. The residence of a legal entity is their official headquarter's location. In criminal cases the court is determined by the district where the crime was committed.

The trial in civil cases is divided into *preparation* and *main hearing*. The preparation usually commences with the defendant's submittance of a written report (statement of defense) within a limited period of time. The defendant specifies in the statement whether he/she admits or challenges (does not agree with) the plaintiff's claim. If the defendant challenges the claim he/she must provide the foundation (reasons) for it. Then the defendant should provide the evidence he/she has. If the defendant finds that there are hindrances to the trial, it should be stated in the statement of defense.

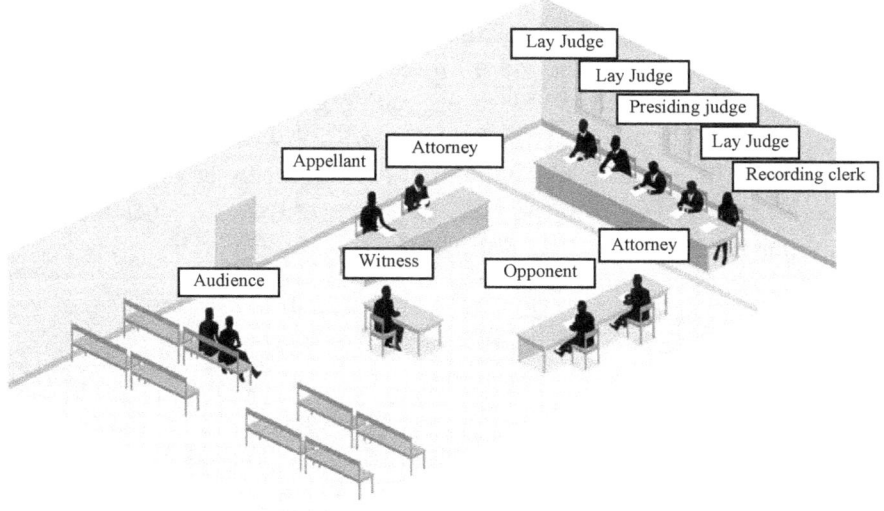

Comment: In most civil cases there are no lay judges, but sometimes there are three judges.

The district court may deliver a judgment by default against a defendant who does not provide a motivated written statement of defence. Judgment by default may also be delivered against a plaintiff who does not want to participate in the process. Also a default judgment is delivered against a party who does not appear at a hearing in the court. Judgment by default usually means that the party who does not respond or fails to appear in court loses the case.

During an *oral preparatory hearing*, the district court tries to get the disputing parties to agree on conciliation, i.e. to agree in some way. If a resolution (settlement) of the dispute does not occur, the court determines the time for the main hearing, i.e. the proper trial.

When preparation is completed, there is eventually the *main hearing*. The parties, witnesses and others who will be questioned are invited to it. In civil cases the court consists of one or three judges: one judge can hear a case the value of which does not exceed a half of the basic amount (22,250 SEK in 2013).

The hearing begins with the plaintiff presenting his claim. Thereafter, the defendant may indicate his/her position. After that the parties account for the background of the dispute and present the facts that they refer to. After this so-called statement of the facts the evidence is presented. The evidence may, for example, include interviews with the parties and witnesses or written evidence. Witnesses have to wait outside the courtroom. They are called in when they are to be questioned. In some cases witnesses are interviewed by telephone. When all evidence of the case has been presented, the parties present their final speeches (closing arguments).

Summons
Statement of defense
Written preparation
Oral preparatory hearing
Possible further written preparation
Possible conciliation
The main hearing
Verdict
Possible appeal

After the main hearing the court (the judges) holds *a private deliberation* in order to jointly decide on the verdict. The verdict is reported to the parties either immediately or within a few weeks. The verdict can in one case mean that the district court approves the claim, i.e. the plaintiff has won and the defendant has thus lost. If the district court does not approve the claim the outcome is the opposite. The party that disagrees with the verdict of the court can appeal to the Court of Appeal. This should be done within three weeks from the time the verdict is reported. Thereafter, the case can be raised in the court of appeal in almost the same way as in the district court. If the appeal is made too late, the verdict is imposed. It means that the case is finally decided and cannot be reopened.

Civil cases with smaller values

A trial procedure can be simplified if the dispute concerns an amount less than half of the base amount, i.e. a little more that 22,000 SEK. These civil cases are referred to as small claims cases. There is only one judge in such a case. The parties do not usually need legal assistance. The court's personnel will give advice to the parties. Whoever loses the case must pay the other party's costs in the form of application fees, travel expenses, collection charges, legal advice and compensation of expenses of witnesses. However, the party that lost the case does not have to pay the other party's attorney's fees that have to be paid in general civil cases.

Conciliation

A dispute can be ended by a conciliation agreement instead of a verdict. A conciliation agreement is the result of conciliation negotiations. They do not differ fundamentally from other agreement negotiations, except for some aspects. The outcome is generally more difficult to assess than in other types of agreements. Usually each party stands for its own legal fees in conciliation.

Conciliation is concluded with a conciliation agreement. Usually it has the following element:

"The above agreement is a final regulation of all the parties' disputes under ... (the agreement at issue)... agreement ".

The above definition is only applicable if the agreement at issue is no longer in effect as a result of the conciliation. If the agreement is still in effect, the formation of what the final conciliation agreement includes can become so complicated that the parties will need the lawyers' help.

Process before a Court

To make it easier for plaintiffs to get through certain types of requirements there are so-called summary proceedings. In this case the handling is performed not in a district court (see below) but in the Swedish Enforcement Authority. The parties are referred to as an *applicant* (*plaintiff*) and a *defendant*. There are three types of summary proceedings:

- *Injunction to pay* which is used when the applicant has a monetary claim, i.e. he wants to be paid.
- *General judicial assistance* that is used when it refers to something other than payment, such as eviction (dispossession) of a tenant who has not paid the rent.
- *Special judicial assistance* is used to return a possession. For example, a possession can be ordered returned when one lent it and did not get back.

In applications for an injunction to pay and general assistance there is no substantial examination, but the application is only delivered to the defendant. The defendant then has an opportunity to *challenge,* which requires the same as in a civil case in a district court. If the defendant fails to object in time, the enforcement authority reports a decision in which the defendant should pay what the plaintiff has requested. The defendant can use the decision as *enforcement* for further actions, such as distress or eviction. If the defendant is dissatisfied with the verdict, he can apply for reclamation in a district court and object (not agree with) to the requirement. In all three cases of summary proceedings the applicant should of course submit documents showing that the claim is just, such as payments, installment contracts, dunning letters (letters of collection), etc.

One who sold goods to a buyer and did not receive full payment can have a monetary claim against the buyer. The seller has no direct right to take back the unpaid and delivered goods, but can demand payment for it. It is the buyer who owns the good now. If the seller, however, has entered an installment agreement with the buyer with a right to return, then it is a different case. If the buyer despite the demands is late with the payments, the seller can apply to the Swedish Enforcement Authority to have the goods returned according to the judicial assistance proceedings.

A distraint sale refers to when the Swedish enforcement authority on behalf of the plaintiff takes possession of and permits the selling of defendant's personal property. Clothing, personal devices, necessary furniture and household equipment and money for daily sustenance are not subject to enforcement and sale. The Enforcement authority may also attach the salary and earnings of a debtor. The debtor has a right to keep the part of his salary enough for the family's living expenses, a so-called reservation amount (normal amount). The amount is defined annually by the National Tax Board.

Case Example

Svea Court of Appeal: ÖÄ7344-02

A single debtor, who worked and lived most of the time in a treatment center for young people, was compelled to make additions to the National Tax Board's reserve amounts from his salary (his salary was 'attached') for the costs of double residence.

Bankruptcy

Those who, despite official payment demand, cannot pay their debts and will not be able to do it for a long period of time, may become bankrupt. Bankruptcy can apply to both private individuals and companies. It means that the assets are taken over by a bankruptcy trustee who uses them to pay off all debts of the person or company. The district court adjudicates bankruptcy cases, upon application by the debtor himself or the creditor, and appoints a bankruptcy trustee. The trustee, usually a lawyer, takes care of the debtor's property, so-called bankrupt estate, and makes a list of the debtor's assets and debts, so-called inventory of the estate. Then the debtor's property is sold and the money is divided among the creditors according to the system of preference, as far as the costs of bankruptcy are paid.

Arbitration

A dispute concerning an agreement does not necessarily have to be judged by a court – it can instead be settled by arbitrators. The parties can agree that any future disputes shall be settled by arbitration instead of litigation in a court of general jurisdiction. This is a common clause of an agreement between companies. It is also possible to arrange arbitration after a dispute has arisen.

Arbitration usually means that the parties appoint arbitrators – one for each party, usually lawyers, who in turn appoint a third one, usually a lawyer or a judge. The latter becomes the arbitration panel chairman. (Sometimes the parties are able to agree on a single arbitrator, who in this case judges by himself.) Arbitration panel's (arbitrators') decision cannot be appealed and is final, unless the panel has made a technical error.

The arbitration procedure is not public, in comparison to the court. There is only one hearing (presentation) of an arbitration claim compared with two or three in the public courts. In that way disputes can be settled faster than by litigating in court, which often takes at least a year and even longer if the verdict is appealed. The costs (arbitrators' and attorneys' fees) are normally paid by the person who loses the case, which has a more significant impact on the economically weaker party. A problem also arises if one party becomes a bankrupt. Then the other party has to pay the full cost of the arbitration regardless of who the "winner" is.

Arbitration Institute

Arbitration Institute of the Stockholm Chamber of Commerce is known in legal circles all over the world. The Institute was founded in 1917 and is an autonomous entity within the Stockholm Chamber of Commerce. In the 1970s the Institute became known as a neutral place for settlement of East-West trade related disputes. The number of cases has grown since then and now the Institute's arbitration operations involve over 40 countries. The Institute has in recent decades developed into one of the major arbitral institutions.

www.sccinstitute.se

Mediation

Mediation is an optional process in which a third party, the mediator, assists and facilitates two or more parties in a conflict. The work is done by dialogue and negotiations in order to try to reach a mutually acceptable agreement. Mediation is used in various fields, including commercial litigation, crime, problems at the working place, family problems, neighborhood feuds, etc.

Mediation is a conflict resolution process by which the disputing parties describe their problems and listen to each other in order to reach an acceptable solution. The mediator assists the parties to achieve a mutually agreeable resolution. It is a procedure that saves time, is confidential and economically efficient. Mediation can be performed by a court or by private arbitration institutions. The Stockholm Chamber of Commerce has a Mediation Institute.

Checkpoint Chapter 3

Explain briefly what is meant by:
A.   Swedish National Board for Consumer Complaints
B.   Parliamentary Ombudsman
C.   Civil case
D.   Summons
E.   Conciliation

F.   Mediation
G.   Judgement by default
H.   Preparation
I.   Main hearing
J.   Civil cases with smaller values (small claims cases)
K.   Legal assistance
L.   Bankruptcy

4

Procedural Law - Criminal Case

Criminal Case

A criminal case originates when a crime is allegedly committed under the Penal Code or other penal provision that may impose punishment. It may for example refer to violent crimes and theft, drug crimes, tax offenses and serious car-related crimes. When there is a suspicion of a crime it is up to the police to investigate suspicions in a so-called *preliminary investigation*. According to the Code of Judicial Procedure the *prosecutor* is responsible for the investigation of more complicated cases and decides whether the case must be passed on to the court.

Crimes do not need to be prosecuted in court if they do not concern serious crime. Examples of such cases can include speeding, driving without a seat belt fastened and smuggling of a non-serious nature. The prosecutor may instead impose an *order of summary punishment* and police can issue *on-the-spot fines* for minor offenses. The injunction means that the suspect must pay a penalty depending on the crime. If the injunction is approved by the suspect, it is regarded as a verdict. On-the-spot fines do not need to be approved in writing. It is enough to pay the fine.

The police may not report a suspected crime by a so-called report concession. The reason for that may be that the offense is insignificant or that it is difficult to make clear whether there was a crime under the circumstances. Report concession may apply only to crimes that result in a fine as a penalty.

Arrest and Detention

A person suspected of a crime may be *detained* by the police. The detention is a deprivation of liberty while the decision on the *arrest* is being made. The decision is made by a prosecutor and is valid until arrest or until the person is released. An arrest means that the police may detain the suspect for up to three days for questioning.

If there is a risk that the suspect may hinder the investigation, commit another crime (risk of relapse into crimes), or leave the jurisdiction, for example, for another country (risk of escape), the prosecutor may apply to the district court for a *detention* permit. It means that the suspect is placed into custody which usually is in a police station. There should be a relatively strong basis for the court's decision on detention. If a crime is of a gross nature, the suspect must be detained, i.e. crimes that impose a penalty of imprisonment for at least two years.

The detention hearing before the court must take place within four days. The suspect may either be *reasonably suspected* of a crime or be suspected *on the basis of probable cause*, which is a stronger finding. Indictment is then normally brought up within two weeks from the detention order. Otherwise, the new detention hearing must be held.

The Prosecutor Makes Decisions on Prosecution

The preliminary investigation will give the prosecutor the evidence that can form the basis for prosecution of the suspect. If the prosecutor considers that the suspect should be prosecuted, he submits an application for summons to the district court. The application for summons must contain:

- Description of the crime (statement of the criminal act)
- Crime classification (such as drink-driving, robbery or assault)
- Applicable law clauses (the legal rules in e.g. Penal Code that describe the crime)
- The evidence the prosecutor can refer to (e.g. witnesses, medical certificates, photos, etc.)

The prosecutor is a party in the case and has to prove that the suspect has committed the crime. It is never the suspect who must prove his innocence.

Personal Case Study

The district court may, if it is necessary to select the proper sanction, obtain the report of the Probation and Parole Authority that is based on a personal investigation result. The report includes a review of the defendant's personal data and a proposed sanction.

A personal case study can be supplemented by a limited medical examination of the mental condition of the accused. In the medical certificate the doctor (a forensic psychiatrist) states his opinion whether there is a need for a more detailed examination of the accused. A medical certificate may also contain an assessment whether the accused must be submitted for forensic psychiatric care.

If the doctor considers it necessary, the court may in some cases decide on a so-called psychiatric examination. Such an examination may only be decided if the accused has admitted his guilt or if there is strong evidence that he is guilty. This means that if the accused denies his guilt the district court must call for the main hearing and settle the question of guilt before reporting the decision on a psychiatric evaluation.

When the investigation is completed, the district court calls for the main hearing during which the sentence is determined.

The Main Hearing in Criminal Cases

The judicial procedure takes place in the form of an oral *main hearing (trial)* which will determine whether the accused has committed the crime that the prosecutor claimed in the application for the summons or not. A prosecutor, a plaintiff (the victim of the crime), a suspect (defendant), a defence lawyer, a judge and lay judges, recording clerks and witnesses are present at the main hearing. In addition, there may be an audience present in the court room, in the same manner as in civil cases.

The main hearing begins in the district court with the announcement of the case, and after that the parties and witnesses are invited into the court room. The presiding judge begins with the attendance check, i.e. he finds out whether everyone has arrived. If someone who has been called to come to the hearing is absent, the hearing must be cancelled and postponed to a later date. In some cases, the court can hold the trial even if the defendant has not appeared. If the presiding judge finds that there is no obstacle to holding the hearing, the witnesses may leave the court room in order to be called in when it's time to listen to them.

The prosecutor claims that the accused should be convicted of the crime by reading the description of the crime that is stated in the application for summons. The prosecutor can also make claims for damages on the plaintiff's (victim's) behalf. The defendant is asked if he or she admits or denies guilt in the crime alleged by the prosecutor. If damages are claimed the defendant is asked if he or she agrees to pay for them.

The prosecutor presents *the particulars of claim* where he or she states the opinion on how the crime has taken place. Usually the prosecutor also reviews the documentary evidence, such as medical certificates, drawings or accounting material. Then the plaintiff is heard and tells about what he or she believes has happened and answers questions. Thereafter, the defendant is heard and can give his version of what has happened. Witnesses are called in one by one and heard after they swear an oath to tell the truth.

Personal background (personal details) is reported by the presiding judge or by the person who takes the minutes of the main hearing.

Deliberations and Voting

After the main hearing the presiding judge and the lay judges hold deliberations, i.e. discuss how the district court should adjudicate the case. During the deliberations it is determined whether the defendant should be convicted of the crime stated in the application for summons and what the case outcome will be. The court also determines other issues, such as damages and costs of the legal procedure (mainly costs of the defence).

Deliberations begin with the presiding judge's presentation of the facts and the content of the legal rules involved. This is followed by a discussion in which all have both a right and duty to express their opinion. As a rule, the court members agree on the adjudication. If someone has a dissenting opinion, there should be a voting. The presiding judge and the lay judges have a vote. First they vote on the question of guilt, i.e. whether the defendant is determined to be guilty for the crime and how the case will be settled. The court votes, for example, whether the crime is to be regarded as a theft or a less serious crime - shoplifting. After the court determines the outcome, the members vote on the sentence.

The main rule for voting is the majority decision. If the votes are equal, the penalty is considered to be most commuted. If neither of the penalties can be considered as less serious or less severe, the presiding judge has a casting vote. All members have to vote. If someone has a dissenting opinion, he has the right to dissent, or "be variant". The dissent or disagreement together with motivation are recorded in the minutes and reported to the parties together with the verdict. If the verdict is appealed, the district court forwards the decision and the materials of the case together with the dissenting opinion to the Court of Appeal.

Question of Guilt

Every legal rule on crime contains a clause that describes the criminal actions and a clause that tells what type of punishment may be caused by the crime. When the question of guilt is being settled, the court investigates the actions made by the accused that correspond to the description of the crime.

However, it is not enough to know that defendant's actions correspond with the crime description in the law. In order to be considered as a crime, it is normally required that the accused acted *intentionally* (dolus). This means that he must have acted willfully.

However, he does not need to have realized that he committed a crime. Some crimes do not require intention in order to punish the offender. For such crimes, the statement of *carelessness* (culpa), or negligence, is enough for punishment.

The requirement of intention means that the court has to judge the criminal's intentions during the crime. It is obvious that such adjudications can be difficult to make.

Evaluation of Evidence

The prosecutor is the one who must prove that the accused has committed the crime, and must therefore come up with (allege) evidence showing the defendant's guilt. The evidence can consist of oral hearings of victims and witnesses or those who know anything about the incident. The evidence may also consist of medical certificates of plaintiffs' injuries or sketches of how a car accident happened.

If the accused denies the guilt the court must consider whether the evidence is sufficient for conviction. The court does not need to state with the absolute certainty that the accused has committed the crime, but there must be a very high degree of probability that the crime was committed. It is usually expressed in the way that the court may only find a defendant guilty for a crime if it is "beyond reasonable doubt" that the accused is guilty.

The court will try to determine whether the accused, the plaintiff or the witnesses are telling the truth or whether any of the information they provided is inaccurate (incorrect). Typically, the court begins with considering various factors that may be important to assess the credibility of the narrative. It can for instance apply to the narrator's:

- relationship to the accused (friends, enemies, victims, etc.)
- possibility of observations (distance, lighting, etc.)
- experience of the event (shocked by the event, engaged in the event, etc.)

In the process of reaching a judgment, the court will be open to various interpretations of fact by the narrator because the person being heard may be mistaken or can deliberately lie. The court must e.g. answer questions as to whether the plaintiff in a case of assault could have been injured in any other way or whether in a case of theft someone else took the property or it simply got lost.

The narratives are considered together with any documentary evidence that supports any of the narratives. After all evidence has been studied, the court can form an overall picture of how strong the evidence is. The main rule is if the evidence is contradictory and the court is not convinced that the accused committed the crime, the accused should "rather be released than imprisoned".

SUMMARY

- It is the prosecutor who must prove that the accused is guilty.

- If the accused denies his guilt, it is an important task for the court to evaluate the facts claimed by the prosecutor.

- Evidence evaluation means that the court seeks to assess the evidence in different parts separately and then obtain a whole picture.

- If the court members are in doubt, the accused should "rather be released that imprisoned".

Verdict

The *verdict* is reported immediately after the trial or later at a specified date, usually in a few weeks. If the prosecutor or the defendant wants to *appeal the verdict* to the court of appeal, it must be done within three weeks. If there will be no appeal, the *sentence becomes final*.

Appeal Petition to the Court of Appeal

The district court's verdict can be appealed to the Court of Appeal. The party or parties who are dissatisfied (complainants) with verdict are able to submit a written appeal to the district court. In the appeal petition the dissatisfied party states how he/she wants the district court's decision to be changed and the reason why it needs to be changed. The appellant must also specify what evidence he wishes to invoke, for example, interviewing of witnesses and victims or certificates of various kinds. The district court then sends the appeal and all the documents of the case to the court of appeal.

In many cases, however, the court of appeal requires a review permit in order to take a case up on appeal (see Chapter 2). If the accused is sentenced only to a fine the review permit is required. If the accused is acquitted, the prosecutor must have a review permit to be able to appeal. A review permit can also be issued if the district court's decision seems to be completely wrong or if there is a so-called precedent interest.

Even in the court of appeal a case must be prepared before it can be settled. Some criminal cases are settled in the court of appeal with the lower court's transcript being evaluated only by legally qualified judges while other criminal cases are decided after an oral hearing. The court of appeal sends the appeal petition to the opposing party of the case to enable him to have the opportunity to respond to what is stated in the appeal petition and present new evidence. The written response to the appeal petition given by the opposing party is called a reply. The reply is then sent to the appellant for information.

Typically, a case in the court of appeal is ready for the main hearing when the appellant is aware of the other party's reply. The district court generally ensures that the required personal investigation results are present, and also appoints a public defender. Sometimes the Court of Appeal, however, has to supplement the personal investigation of the accused. If the accused has not had a public defender in the district court, the court of appeal can appoint a public defender to assist the accused in the court of appeal.

Before the hearing, the Court of Appeal sends a so-called main hearing memorandum to all the judges and even lay judges who will participate. The memorandum contains the district court's verdict and important documentary evidence referred to. Moreover, there is a schedule of the hearing: everyone is called at a scheduled time. Sometimes a legal investigation is done as well as research into the various legal cases that can be relevant and of interest to the case on appeal.

An important principle that should be emphasized is that the court of appeal cannot adjudicate someone who appealed a district court's verdict to a penalty stricter than the one he got in the district court. However, if both the convicted party and the prosecutor file an appeal, the court of appeal is free to impose a more severe penalty.

The Main Hearing

Lay judges participate in the main hearings of the criminal cases in which the verdict may be expected to be more serious than a fine. The court of appeal becomes a so-called quorum of three legally qualified judges and two lay judges. If one of the judges or one of the lay judges is unable to take part after the trial has commenced, the court is nevertheless legally competent. More than four judges and three lay judges cannot participate.

The main hearing in court of appeal is generally the same as the main hearing in district court. An important difference of course is that a decision has already been imposed in the case. The verdict is read out at the beginning of the trial. Another difference is that the contents of the appeal petition are the starting point for what the court of appeal will examine at the main hearing. For example, an accused may have been convicted of both theft and assault by the district court. In the appeal petition he can state that he accepts that he has been convicted of theft but he considers himself innocent of assault. So the court of appeal must only consider whether he is guilty of assault. The plaintiff and witnesses are usually not heard again; instead the video-recorded examination made by the district court is played.

Deliberations and Voting

Like the district court, the court of appeal holds their deliberations immediately after the main hearing in which the judges discuss and agree on adjudication. As a rule at the beginning of deliberations a procurator fiscal (see Chapter about Swedish Courts) explains what has been presented during the main hearing and reviews the content of the legal rules to be applied. After that, the case is discussed. Everyone is obliged to express their opinion. As a rule the members talk in a certain order: the lay judges speak at the end. Usually, the judges agree on the verdict. If someone has a dissenting opinion, a special voting is performed with practically the same principles as in the district court (see section about deliberations in district court).

A Crime or just an Accident?

An action that causes loss or damage to property or another person may not necessarily be a crime or result in the imposition of liability for damages. It can also be an accident that no one can be blamed for or can be due to minor negligence that still is not a crime. In order to be a crime the action first and foremost is required to be regulated by law and it must be comprised of *intention* (on purpose), *dolus* in Latin, or due to unacceptable *negligence* (carelessness), *culpa* in Latin.

But this is still not enough for it to be a crime. In addition, there must be a direct and proven connection between the action and the loss or damage, *adekvat kausalitet* (adequate causality) in Latin. Circumstances (dispositive facts) should therefore point out that the action has caused loss or damage, which is supported by evidence. Together with a rule of law and evidence, this gives a correct result, e.g. a punishment. Requirements (conditions) for an action to be judged as a crime are called *prerequisites*.

Dispositive facts ---Rule of Law ----- Evidence ----- Sequence of Law

Case Example

Supreme Court: B2328-05

A nurse, who accidentally mixed an infusion solution for an infant that was ten times stronger than prescribed, which thereby caused the child's death, was accused of infliction of another person's death and adjudged to a suspended sentence together with day-fines of 50-120 SEK. With concern for the patients' safety and confidence in the health care, the nurse's action with an overall assessment of the facts must be considered as liable to punishment because it involves penal negligence. For that reason, the nurse cannot escape liability for manslaughter.

A crime may occur without having caused losses or damage. It refers to an action that leads to *hazard* that can cause losses or damage, for example by reckless driving or carelessness with fire.

Even planning of a crime can be a criminal act, for example, preparation for a murder or attempt of theft. This cannot be applied to all types of crimes, for example, an attempt of shop lifting is not a criminal act. Shoplifting is considered a crime when the goods are carried out of the store, i.e. without being paid for and with alarm loops.

Assistance in committing a crime can also be considered as a crime, e.g. assistance in assault.

Self-Defense - not Offense

The Penal Code allows exempting a person from liability for a criminal act if it happened in the form of so-called self-defense. Under certain circumstances one can commit a criminal act without becoming liable according to the following excerpt from the Penal Code:

An act becomes criminal if the act is unjustifiable with respect to circumstances when one applied more violence "than it was necessary" (so-called excessive self-defense).

Case Example

Göta Court of Appeal: B421-97

A couple of boys threw crackers from embankment down on people passing by. A man that came up to them and caught two of the boys and threatened to throw them down from the embankment if they did not stop was released from liability for an illegal threat on the basis of the right to self-defence.

Whom Can the Criminal Law Concern?

The Swedish criminal law concerns crimes committed in Sweden, both by Swedish and foreign citizens. Swedish residents can also be sentenced for crimes they committed in other countries. It means that a person serving his sentence in another country can be transferred to Sweden to continue to serve his sentence there. The person gets the foreign sentence period credited in Sweden.

Wednesday, November 29, 2000

Committee on Justice corrects an error in the Penal Code

Committee on Justice has taken the initiative to correct the technical legal error in the Penal Code which recently had been discovered during an ongoing trial. Text of the law was amended so as to be possible to judge a person for a serious crime in Sweden even if the person has already been accused of the same crime abroad. The Parliament decided on the matter on December 5. The Act was enforced on December 8.

Checkpoint Chapter 4

Explain briefly what is meant by:

A.   Criminal case

B.   Arrest

C.   Detention

D.   Preliminary investigation

E.   Main hearing (trial)

F.   Plaintiff

G.   Dolus

H.   Culpa

I.   The self-defense

J.   Adequate causality

5

Criminal Law

Criminal law is the part of jurisprudence relating to crime and its sanctions, as opposed to civil law which among other things deals with agreements between the parties. Criminal law deals with the matters that the government wants to prevent. Such matters are theft, robbery, assault, fraud, arson, etc. The central criminal laws in Sweden are found in the Penal Code.

The View on Crime and Punishment

Deterrence and retaliation

Until the end of the 1600s sentences have been imposed out of cruelty. Both tortures and death penalties occurred like public flogging. Another form of punishment was cutting off a criminal's body part, i.e. mutilation. Pillory was used to immobilize a criminal, so that he had to stand or sit and be put to shame in public. The purpose of punishment was primarily to deter from crime, so-called general prevention, but also to be a just revenge for the victim, so-called retaliation.

A version of retaliation is the so-called Talion principle which means that the offender must be subjected to the same damage as he caused. Another way of saying it is "Eye for an eye, tooth for a tooth." Talion principle still exists in the Swedish law of damages: those who were injured under certain circumstances may be entitled to correspondent compensation from the person who caused the injury.

Enlightenment

The Enlightenment was a philosophical and political movement that advocated men's equal value before the society and before the law. It emerged at the beginning of 1700s originating in England and France and during 1800s it became the base for a more modern view on punishment, the so-called classical criminal law schools. They included three main principles:

- Legality (compliance with the law)
- Egality (equality, equal opportunities, i.g. before the law)
- Proportionality (the seriousness of a penalty is assessed depending on severity of the offense)

Treatment Ideology

In the mid-1900s a new concept in the view on punishment was created - treatment ideology. Criminality was explained by social background factors and experiences. Penalty for a crime would be adapted to the individual's particular needs, which among others led to new types of sanctions such as suspended sentences and probation. This view was so-called individually preventive, i.e. it tried to prevent further crime by treating individuals, not punishing them.

Neo-Classicism

As a counterbalance to the treatment ideology and to some extent to the criticism of an insufficient focus on the victim the so-called neo-classicism was created, a new approach to punishment. In the assessment of a crime, its culpability is assumed according to a scale used by the courts. Neo-classicism follows similar principles as the classical criminal law school. In the current Swedish system we have a combination of general prevention and individual prevention.

Criminal Acts and Consequences

Anyone who is convicted of a crime must get some form of punishment (penalty). For example, one can be forced to pay *fines* or sit in *jail* depending on the seriousness of the crime committed. Examples of other forms of sanctions are *electronic surveillance* ("electronic footcuffs"), *conditional sentences, probation* and *special care for addicts and the mentally ill.* The *correctional treatment authority* is in charge of these sanctions.

Criminal law covers various types of criminal acts (crimes) which can lead to some form of punishment (penal sanction). This field is governed mainly by the *Criminal Code* which is divided into three parts.

- Part One (Chapters 1-2) with the general provisions on crimes and sanctions.

- Part Two (Ch 3-24) with the definition of various forms of crime and possible sanctions, i.e. a type of crime catalog.

- Part Three (Chapters 25-36) that describes various sanctions, fines, imprisonment, conditional sentences, probation, etc.

In addition to the Penal Code there are also so-called *special criminal laws* that regulate road traffic offenses, drug offenses, weapons crimes, terrorist crimes and others.

There are usually no penalties in the *civil law* even if a behavior would be "contrary to the law." Instead there may be other consequences, for example compensation to a contracting party in the form of a new delivery, price reduction, compensation for damages, etc. Even if a behavior involves "breaking the law" it is not considered a criminal liability in the civil law. However, it can happen that a civil action is so serious that it turns into a crime according to the Penal Code, e.g. fraud, unlawful threat, etc.

A common feature of the criminal law and the civil law is that the person who caused the losses or damages may be *liable for them.* It is not a punishment in the ordinary sense but an obligation to pay compensation to the victim for all damage, for example, destroyed or lost property, personal injury, etc. Liability for damages is regulated either by law on damages or by a civil agreement. In the criminal law it is the *injured party* who can be entitled to compensation.

In certain specialized areas, including market legislation, an act can cause a so-called penalty payment adjudged by the court if the act is repeated. A penalty is thus a form of fines to be paid on a repeated violation of the law.

Different Types of Crimes

Crimes against a person (chapter 3-7 and 16-17 of the Penal Code)

It refers to crimes against people, including assault, unlawful threat, harassment, sexual crimes and murders, penalties for which are the most serious - up to 18 years of imprisonment (for murder).

Capital offence (felony) (Chapter 8-12 of the Penal Code)

Capital offence means that the victims suffer from a financial loss caused by a crime. It can be theft, fraud, receiving stolen property and robbery with imprisonment for at most 10 years (gross robbery).

Crimes against public and state (Chapter 13-20 of the Penal Code)

Crimes against the public and the state are not exactly directed against an individual, but an individual can be affected indirectly. Examples include persecution of an ethnic group, riot, forgery and arson with imprisonment up to life term (for arson).

Violation of special criminal laws (including road traffic offenses act and drugs offence act)

Examples of offenses within the special criminal law are road traffic offenses and drug offenses with imprisonment for at most 10 years for drug offense.

Violation of intellectual property laws (including copyright law, patent law and trademark law)

Crimes that include violation of copyright of literature, music, movies, computer programs, trade names, patents, trademarks and designs.

Crimes against Persons (Chapters 3-7 and 16-17 of the Penal Code)

Violent Crimes

According to the National Council for Crime Prevention (BRÅ) this category includes murder, manslaughter, infanticide and assault causing or not causing another person's death (Penal Code, Chapter 3), gross violation of integrity and violation of women's integrity (Penal Code, Chapter 4), rape including gross rape (Penal Code, Chapter 6), robbery including gross robbery (Penal Code, Chapter 8) and violence against a public servant (Penal Code, Chapter 17)

Murder usually implies that the offender planned to kill his victim and then implemented it. If the intention was to kill, but there was no direct planning, it counts as manslaughter or assault with a fatal outcome (Penal Code, Chapter 3)

The Punishment for Murder and Others Crimes

On 1 July 2009 the scale of penalties for murder was changed from ten years or life-term imprisonment to imprisonment for at least ten years and at most 18 years or a life-term. The raised maximum penalty to 18 years has been in force since July 1, 2009 and applies also to other crimes for which there is a mandatory sentence of both a stated period of time and a lifetime, such as kidnapping, gross arson, gross sabotage, gross espionage, international crime, genocide and terrorism. Fixed-term imprisonment may be determined for at most 18 years even in cases with multiple crimes or relapse of particularly serious crime. People under 21 who have committed murder or another of the aforementioned crimes may be sentenced to imprisonment for at most 14 years instead of ten years as it was earlier.

Crimes of assault and gross assault (Penal Code chapter 3) constitute the majority of violent crimes reported to the police in Sweden according to BRÅ. The penalty for assault is a fine or imprisonment for at most two years, if the crime is gross, the punishment can be imprisonment for at most ten years.

Case Example

The bus driver who had hit a 15-year-old at Orminge center was punished with a fine.

Two 15-year-old boys were going to downtown to buy new hockey sticks. They came late to the bus, which had already started. One of the guys kicked easily on the door, but he should not have done this. The driver stopped the bus, got out and gave him a box on the ear. Then they both got on the bus and took a ride to the Slussen station. The driver denies the events, but the district court believes the boys' opinion. The driver is sentenced for assault and molestation, and in addition to a day-fine of 6,000 SEK and to pay 5,000 SEK for the injury to the boy he slapped.

- Besides this penalty, the driver will not be allowed to continue driving. We will do an investigation and see if it affects his employment. We will make a decision within the next few days, said a representative of the employer.

Crimes Caused by Carelessness and Negligence

This crime category includes negligence and carelessness causing another person's death, bodily injuries, disease or danger (Penal Code, Chapter 3) and carelessness endangering the public (Penal Code, Chapter 13). The penalty for carelessness causing another person's death is a fine or imprisonment for at most two years; if the crime is gross, the imprisonment for at most six years shall be imposed.

Threats, Violation of Integrity and Violation of Liberties Crimes

This category includes all crimes in the Penal Code Chapter 4-5, threat or assault to a public servant (Penal Code, Chapter 17), unlawful discrimination (Penal Code, Chapter 16), agitation against an ethnic group (Penal Code, Chapter 16), violation of ban on visitors (SFS 1988:688), violent resistance (Penal Code, Chapter 17), arbitrary conduct concerning a child (Penal Code, Chapter 7).

Gross Violation of a Woman's Integrity

Gross violation of a woman's integrity (Penal Code, Chapter 4) is a situation when a man commits repeated violations of integrity such as assault, illegal threats, harassment, trespassing and sexual constraint against a woman with whom he has or had a close marriage-like relationship. The penalty is imprisonment for at least six months and at most six years.

Unlawful Threat and Molestation

Unlawful threats and molestation are stated in Chapter 4 of the Penal Code. The penalty is a fine or imprisonment for at most one year.

Breach of Domiciliary Peace

A person who unlawfully intrudes in another person's home or garden commits the breach of domiciliary peace and a person who unlawfully intrudes in a factory, office, etc. shall be sentenced for unlawful intrusion under Chapter 4 of the Penal Code. The sentence for this is a fine, or if the crime is gross, imprisonment for at most two years shall be imposed.

Defamation

A person who points out someone as being a criminal or as having a reprehensible way of living or otherwise furnishes information intended to cause exposure to the disrespect of others, shall be sentenced for defamation to a fine (Penal Code Chapter 5). If the crime is gross, the accused can be sentenced for gross defamation to a fine or imprisonment for at most two years. In assessing whether the crime is gross, special consideration shall be given to whether the information, because of its content or the scope of its dissemination of otherwise, was calculated to bring about serious damage.

Case Example

Gross defamation: Spreading of offending movies

Teenage boys were convicted of gross defamation. They spread movies via Microsoft's MSN. The films contained images of young girls and lyrics of an offensive and sexual character. The boys had to pay a total of between 140,000 SEK and 600,000 SEK for damages.

Sexual Crimes

This category includes rape, sexual coercion, sexual exploitation, sexual harassment, indecent exposure, procuring, seduction of youth and child pornography crimes (Penal Code, Chapter 6). The sentence for rape is imprisonment for at most four years, and if the crime is gross the imprisonment for at least two years and at most six years shall be imposed. The penalty for sexual coercion is imprisonment for at most two years, and if the crime is gross the imprisonment for at least six months and at most six years shall be imposed.

Case Example

The sentence was changed to gross procuring

The district court sentenced a 39-year-old man to a one year's imprisonment for procuring. The court of appeal changed the sentence to a gross procuring and increased the punishment to two years imprisonment. The man was sentenced for having promoted sexual relations with five women prostitutes, including his own wife, to hundreds of men.

Human trafficking for sexual purposes (Penal Code, Chapter 4) causes imprisonment for a gross crime for at least four years and at most eighteen years, for a minor crime – for at most six years of imprisonment. According to BRÅ, sexual crimes committed in private places are reported less frequently to the police than crimes committed in a public place. Crimes where the victim and perpetrator are acquainted with each other are reported less frequently than if they are unfamiliar, and less serious crimes are reported less frequently that gross crimes.

Case Example

Extracts from the Supreme Court's Verdict

"Even if the act which XX has done is gross, it indicates that it is of a kind as referred to in the third paragraph of § 1 of Chapter 6 of the Penal Code. It must be taken into special consideration whether it was a sequence that lasted during a short time and that XX had discontinued his action as soon as YY woke up and made it clear she was not interested in sexual intercourse. Violence or threat of violence did not take place and beyond the infringement that the abuse itself implies, the act had no humiliating or degrading elements. XX shall be convicted of rape under the third paragraph of § 1 Chapter 6 of the Criminal Code".

A crime of buying sex means payment for a sexual service and refers to a person who obtains or attempts to obtain casual sexual relations (Penal Code, Chapter 6). The penalty is imprisonment for at most six months.

Example

A top director was convicted of buying sex.

The man is said to have had a contact with a prostitute on Malmskillnadsgatan in Stockholm to whom he offered 1,500 SEK for massage and oral sex, reported Aftonbladet. But police investigators followed the car to Sveavägen where the man was arrested. The man denies buying sex and says he just asked if he and the prostitutes would "do something". He was convicted in the District Court to 50,000 SEK in fines. The 55 year old director is a board member in 20 companies and works as a CEO in one.

Felonies (Chapter 8-12 of the Penal Code)

Theft, Robbery and Other Crimes of Stealing

This category includes theft, robbery and gross robbery (Penal Code, Chapter 8), receiving (Penal Code, Chapter 9), as well as shoplifting in the stores, department stores, commercial showrooms (Penal Code, Chapter 8). A burglary is a break-in into someone's home and considered as a gross theft (Penal Code Chapter 8). The sentence for theft is imprisonment for at most two years, for shoplifting – a fine or imprisonment for at most six months. The sentence for robbery is imprisonment for at least one year and at most six years, and if the crime is gross, imprisonment for at least four years and at most ten years shall be imposed. Robbery contains violence or threats of violence. The sentence for receiving of stolen goods is imprisonment for at most two years. Receiving of stolen goods is an awareness of the sale or disposal of stolen goods.

Case Example

Circumstances turned shoplifting into theft

The jeans cost 800 SEK and the crime could therefore be assessed as shoplifting. But the man removed the alarm tag and put it in another pair of jeans which he put back on the table. This was considered gross and the crime was adjudicated as theft.

Car, Bike, etc. Theft

Vehicle theft (Penal Code, Chapter 8) is often considered as a form of arbitrary conduct because it cannot be verified if the culprit appropriates the vehicle and keeps it or if it's only a temporary "borrowing". The sentence for theft is a fine or imprisonment for at most two years, if the crime is gross the imprisonment for at least six months and at most four years shall be imposed.

Fraud and Crimes on Falsification

This category includes violations of Chapters 9 and 14 of the Penal Code. Examples are various forms of fraud, falsification of documents (identity papers' falsification) as well as signature falsification and counterfeiting currency. The sentence for gross fraud and gross falsification is a fine or imprisonment for at most six years, and if the crime is a fraudulent conduct and is regarded as petty a fine or imprisonment for at most six months shall be imposed.

The crime statistics report on many forms of fraud, such as fraud with credit cards or debit cards, frauds when a person did not pay for hotel, restaurant, taxi, bus, or fraud against insurance offices or insurance companies. A significant part of the reported crimes is listed as "other fraud".

Financial Crime

Financial crime is not a part of the Penal Code - it is a generic term. For example, embezzlement, withholding property, and breaches of trust against a principal (Penal Code, Chapter 10), crimes against creditors (Penal Code, Chapter 11), violation of law on taxes (SFS 1971:69), violation against insider act (SFS 2000:1086), the companies act (1975:1385 SS) and against the ban on business operations (SFS 1986:436).

Sometimes financial crimes are described as "profit crimes that occur in business operations." Financial crime is usually detected and reported by government authorities, such as National Tax Board, Swedish Enforcement Agency, Swedish Customs and Swedish Economic Crime Authority.

Crimes Inflicting Damage (including Arson)

This category includes everything from graffiti to other damages (Penal Code, Chapter 12) and arson (Penal Code, Chapter 13). Crimes inflicting damage are often committed together with other crimes, such as theft and crime of violence. The sentence for crimes inflicting damage is a fine or imprisonment for at most one year, and if the crime is gross, imprisonment for at most four years shall be imposed.

Crimes against Public and State (Chapter 13-15 of the Penal Code)

Carelessness Endangering the Public

A person who deals carelessly with fire and explosives shall be sentenced for carelessness endangering the public to a fine or imprisonment for at most six months. (Penal Code, Chapter 13).

Falsification

A person who falsifies a document, such as identifications or certificates, shall be sentenced for documents falsification to imprisonment for at most two years. If the offense is gross, imprisonment for at least six months and at most six years shall be imposed. Petty crimes of falsification of a document are imposed to a fine or imprisonment for at most six months.

Crimes against the State (Chapter 16-20 of the Penal Code)

Crimes against Public Order

A person who violently stands up against an authority shall be sentenced to instigation and conduction of a riot (Penal Code, Chapter 16). The sentence for the instigator and conductor is imprisonment for at most four years, and for another participant - a fine or imprisonment for at most two years.

Agitation against a National or Ethnic Group

Agitation against a national or ethnic group (Penal Code, Chapter 16) is legally complex, because it affects freedom of speech and its limits. In many cases it may be difficult to determine if an opinion is an agitation against a national or ethnic group or not. The sentence for agitation against a national or ethnic group is a fine or imprisonment for at most two years, and if the crime is gross, imprisonment for at least six months and at most four years shall be imposed.

Violence to Public Servant

Violence to public servant means that a person who, by violence or threat of violence, attacks anyone in his exercise of public authority or compels him to perform or to prevent him from performing an official act (Penal Code, Chapter 17). The sanction for violence or threat to public servant is a fine or imprisonment for at most four years if the crime is gross.

Interference in a Judicial Matter and other Crimes against Public Activity

A person who by violence or threat tries to prevent witnesses from performing in court can be sentenced for interference in judicial matter (Penal Code, Chapter 17). The sentence is imprisonment for at most four years, and if the crime is gross, imprisonment for at least two and at most eight years shall be imposed.

Other crimes against public activities of this group of crimes include bribery (bribery), improper activity at election and accepting an improper reward for voting, violation the privacy of suffrage, protection of criminals, aiding escape, violation of official order, obstructing a functionary of the ordinances and pretence of public office. All of these crimes are listed in Chapter 17 of the Penal Code.

Environmental Crimes (animals and nature)

These group of crimes include spreading of / handling of/ negligence with poison / contagious substance (Penal Code, Chapter 13), violation of the Environmental Code (SFS 1998:808), violations of the Law on Prevention of Pollution from Ships (SFS 1980:424), the Hunting Act (SFS 1987:259) and the Fishing Act (SFS1993: 787).

Sentences for these crimes are stated in the Environmental Code, Chapter 29. When environmental crimes are discovered by the regulatory authority they are obligated to give notice of the suspects to the courts.

Violation of Special Criminal Laws

Weapons Crime

This category includes illegal possession of guns, revolvers, submachine guns, hunting guns, other weapons and other violations of the Gun Laws (SFS 1996:67), as well as unlawful possession of knives and other dangerous objects covered by the Act on Prohibition of knives and other dangerous objects (SFS 1988:254). The crimes are detected and registered usually when someone is apprehended by the police in connection with other types of crimes, including assault and robbery.

Certain Traffic Offences

The law on certain traffic offences (SFS 1951:649) includes gross negligence in traffic, illegal driving (including gross), drunken driving (including gross), drunken driving under the influence of drugs and hit-and-run driving, i.e. escaping from the accident site without reporting. A careless and inattentive driver can be sentenced today-fines for careless driving. If a person is guilty for gross negligence or shows obvious disregard for the lives of property of others while driving a motor vehicle, he shall be sentenced for gross careless driving and imposed an imprisonment for at most two years.

Tax Offence

A person who deliberately gives false information to the authorities or fails to submit declarations, statement of earnings and tax deductions or other required information, and thus causes incorrect tax calculations, shall be sentenced for tax offence and imposed imprisonment for at most two years. If the tax offense is considered gross, imprisonment for at least six months and at most six years shall be imposed. In assessing if the crime is gross special consideration shall be given to whether it involved large sums of money or whether the offender used falsified documents and fallacious accounting.

Smuggling and Customs Offence

A person is committing a smuggling crime when he imports goods into the country which are covered by a specific prohibition or importing conditions, and does not declare the goods in the customs. A person, who does not declare the goods in the customs, submits an incorrect declaration or does not submit the required declaration and thereby causes the withdrawal of additional taxes or duties from the society, shall be sentenced for customs offence. Both crimes are stated in the Act on Penalties for Smuggling (SFS2000:1225).

Alcohol and Drug Offence

This category includes crimes against Narcotic drugs Act (SFS 1968:64) and the Act on Penalties for Smuggling (SFS2000: 1225), drink driving and driving under the influence of drugs (SFS1951: 649) and violation of the The Act on the Control of Narcotic Drugs (SFS1992: 860).

Alcohol offenses are violations of the Alcohol Law (SFS1994: 1738) that include illegal sales of alcohol products and violation of the law of sale of crude spirit (SFS 1951:649), drink driving and doping offenses (SFS 1991:1969). Drink driving offenses are also reported as traffic crimes.

Financing Terrorism

Penal provisions for financial support of terrorist activities (SFS 2002:444) include sentencing for financing of particularly serious crimes in some cases.

Violation of Intellectual Property Law

Violation of intellectual property law is violation of rights to among other things literature, music, movies, computer programs, trade names, patents, trademarks and design. The laws governing the protection of intellectual property are so-called intellectual property laws, including copyright in literary and artistic works, trademark law, patent law, design law and business law. Illegal use of another person's text, piece of music, movie, computer software, trademarks, designs and trade names is a crime. Copying and selling of a copyright protected product or otherwise making it available to others, e.g. through file sharing, is considered a violation of the law. The sentence for a violation of intellectual property is usually a fine or imprisonment for at most two years.

Copywrite owners can, in some cases with support of the law, obtain information about those who abetted in the crime against copyrighted material, e.g. computer companies. Such possibility is included in all the laws that protect intellectual property and is based on an EU directive IPRED (Intellectual Property Rights Enforcement Directive).

Attempt, Preparation, Planning and Co-Responsibility for Crimes

Attempted Crimes

Even an attempt of a crime shall in some cases be punishable if is it defined in the Penal Code for a relevant offense.

1 § A person who has begun to commit a crime without bringing it to completion, shall, in cases where specific provisions exist for the purpose, be sentenced for attempting to commit a crime if there was a danger that the act would lead to the completion of the crime or such danger had been precluded only because of fortuitous circumstances.

Punishment for attempt shall be at most what is applicable to a completed crime and not less that imprisonment if the least punishment for the completed crime is imprisonment for two years or more.

Planning of a Crime

Decisions and planning to commit a crime shall in some cases be punishable and classified as preparation or conspiracy to commit a crime according to Chapter 23, § 2 of the Penal Code. By conspiracy is meant that someone plans a crime in collusion with another. The punishment shall be less than the highest for the crime itself and may be less that the lowest limit applicable to the completed crime.

Interrupted participation in criminal activity

A person who discontinued his participation or attempted to prevent a crime can escape punishment for involvement or conspiracy to commit a crime.

§ 3 Responsibility for attempting, preparing or conspiring to commit a crime shall not exist if a person voluntarily, by breaking off the execution of the crime or otherwise, has prevented its completion. Even if the crime was completed, a person who has unlawfully provided the means to that end may not be held criminally responsible for that reason if he has voluntarily prevented the criminal use of the means.

Joint Responsibility for a Crime

Punishment for a crime may be imposed not only on the person who committed it, but also on anyone who is jointly responsible in any way. According to § 4, Chapter 23 of the Penal Code the joint responsibility is defined as instigation or assistance. By instigation is meant that a person actively influenced another person to commit a crime. The punishment for instigation or assistance shall be the same as for the crime itself, but can be reduced if there are mitigating circumstances. A person who only made an attempt to seduce another to commit a crime usually shall not be imposed a punishment.

Terrorist offenses

Since the September 11, 2001 attacks of the World Trade Center in New York, the EU has intensified its struggle against terrorism. A part of that strategy is a so-called Framework Decision adopted in 2002, whereby member countries shall legislate what should be considered as terrorist crimes. After defining the offenses to be counted as terrorism, the punishments for the offences are defined in the legislations of the member states.

Terrorist offences mean that someone commits an act that can cause serious damages and losses to a state or an inter-governmental organization, e.g. murder, vandalism or spreading poison or contagious substances. The crime was introduced to the Swedish legislation in 2003. The punishment shall be imprisonment for at least four years and at most ten years or a life imprisonment, and if a crime is not gross, imprisonment for at least two years and at most six years shall be imposed.

Case Example

Stockholm District Court: Imprisonment for Terrorism

On 14 June 2006 Stockholm District Court, for the second time in Sweden, issued a judgment under the Act (2003:148) on Criminal Responsibility for Terrorist Offences which came into effect on 1 July 2003.

The district court has sentenced NG for an attempted terrorist offense and AF for assistance in the attempt of the crime: NG, equipped with seven bottles with gasoline, so-called Molotov cocktails, tried to explode a venue in Kista which on 13-15 December 2005 which was used for parliamentary elections in Iraq. The district court also sentenced NG, AF and AR for conspiracy to commit a terrorist offence: they decided to burn the main building of Word of Life organization in Uppsala.

NG was sentenced to imprisonment for three years and six months, AF to imprisonment for two years and AR, who was only 19 years old at the time of crime commitment, to imprisonment for eight months. Earlier NG was sentenced for gross doping offenses to imprisonment for four years which had not been enforced by the time of the present offense.

It was stated that the defendants had been strongly influenced by the concept of Mujahedeen and the "romance of violence" that can be associated with the crime. As shown in their chatting history and in the confiscated materials, they have strongly stood against the USA's involvement in Iraq. In connection with their bombing attempt in Kista, AF sent a message on to Swedish media behalf of the NG, in which he stated that the act had been ordered by Al - Qaeda's senior leaders in Sweden. The message included threats such as not to let the sons of pigs, etc. carry out their plans in Iraq.

The decision to set fire to the Word of Life's building in Uppsala arose because the representatives of the Word of Life organization expressed support for Israel in the Palestine conflict. As it was shown the chatting history, the plans of the crime included sending a similar message to the mass media that had been sent in connection with the bombing attempt in Kista.

The district court found that the acts were aimed at intimidating the Swedish civilian population and not just the voting Iraqis in Sweden and the Word of Life's supporters. The district court has also stated that the acts, if they had been accomplished, could have brought serious damage to Sweden. In that context, the district court has also stated that it is fundamental for a democratic state that a parliamentary election must be conducted privately and safely. The district court also stated that a democratic state must protect freedom of the citizens to freely express their opinions and that a failure in that regard can have serious consequences for the state and its citizens.

As a matter of court practice, attempted crimes and conspiracy crimes are usually have less serious sentences than that for the crime itself. The fact that the district court determined that the crimes are attributable to the Act on Criminal Responsibility for Terrorist Offences, not just to attempted crimes and conspiracy offenses: penal code provisions on arson have led decisions on more severe punishments than it may be considered following the practice in these cases. The court's verdict lies within the range claimed by the prosecutor.

The district court's decision means that the rest of the prosecutor's primary claim was approved in all respects.

Source: Swedish Courts (www.domstol.se)

Fighting against terrorism

The Security Service is responsible for fighting against terrorism in Sweden. The service prevents attacks in Sweden or against Swedish interests, or terrorist attacks that are planned in or supported from Sweden. Terrorists should not be able to hide or to collect money for terrorism here. They should not use Sweden as a base for recruitment and logistic support. If a terrorist attack happens in Sweden, the Security Service is responsible for investigating the crime. Such investigations are performed in the form of a prosecution-led investigation – just as in other police investigations. The Security Service also participates in international cooperation against terrorism and in assisting other countries in their preventive work and investigations.

It is extremely important for the Security Service that the person who provides us with information can do it safely and securely. It also explains why the information providers' actions are in secrecy and that details are rarely given about that part of the intelligence work. The Security Service's procedures regarding the actions of the information provider have been reviewed by the Chancellor of Justice (JK - Justitiekanslern) who finds that the Security Service's work with information providers is conducted in an intelligent, unified and secure manner.

Source: www.sakerhetspolisen.se

Example

Man arrested for conspiracy to commit terrorism

Security service arrested a Swedish citizen in the Gothenburg area on Tuesday. The man was suspected of conspiracy to commit terrorist crimes. The man was charged in absentia on the basis of probable cause – suspected of conspiracy to commit a terrorist crime. The Security Service followed the man for some time and the arrest was conducted by personnel from the Security Service.

- He was arrested today in the Gothenburg area due to suspicions about an attack in Somalia, said Security Service's spokesman Patrick Peter to Nyhetskanalen.se.

Patrick Peter told us that, at the moment, the information on investigations is confidential. Therefore, neither the Security Service nor preliminary investigation's head - Agnetha Hilding Qvarnström, the deputy chief prosecutor at the Public Prosecutor's Office for National Security, currently provide any further information.

- I will not give any additional information beyond what is contained in our press release, says Patrick Peter.

Published May 18, 2010 15:59

Determining Sanctions

If the court found that the accused committed a crime, it shall decide what penalty should be imposed. Each legal provision on crimes states what punishment shall follow the crime, so-called imposed penalty. A penalty is imposed according to how gross the crime is in relation to other crimes. For some crimes a fine or imprisonment can be imposed, while for other crimes both fine and imprisonment can be imposed.

Fines (Penal Code, Chapter 25)

Day-fines are often imposed for minor crimes, and are assessed a minimum number of 30 and a maximum of 150 with the number depending on the severity of the offense. The amount of each day-fine is determined by what is reasonable depending on the offender's income. A minimum day-fine is 30 SEK and the highest is 1000 SEK. Day-fines must correspond to one thousandth part of the offender's annual income (in some cases, special deductions are made).

Example

An offender's annual income is 250,000 SEK, the day-fine is then 250,000 / 1,000 = 250 SEK. If the offender is sentenced to 60 day-fines, the total amount of the fine 60 x SEK 250 = SEK 15 000. A summary fine is, unlike a day-fine, a fixed amount of at least 200 SEK and 4,000 SEK at most.

Summary fines are typically imposed for traffic offenses. Examples of reasons for summary fines in traffic are not fastening of a seat belt - SEK 1,500, driving on a red light - SEK 3,000, not using winter tires during the prescribed period -, 200 SEK, driving with studded tires during forbidden period - SEK 500. Parking offence fines ("parking fines") are not a punishment but a fee charged by the parking company or the municipality.

The court must adjudicate according to the range of penalties. If imprisonment is a part of the punishment, the court may instead choose a different, lighter sentence. In some cases the range of penalties can be exceeded, e.g. on multiple crimes or relapses. In other cases the court may deviate from the range of penalties and impose a lighter sentence, for example if a crime is committed by young people.

The main principle is that the sentence is determined by the penal value, i.e. how severe the crime is in an individual case. Penal value is determined with regard to the injury, danger or violation the crime involved. Even the offender's intentions or motives for his actions affect the sentence.

When the penalty value is assessed, the court may consider various aggravating or mitigating circumstances. Thus, it can be aggravating if the offense is against children, and mitigating if the offender was subject to serious provocation. The court must also take into account whether the accused attempted to voluntarily admit his fault, for example by paying for damages, or if he voluntarily turned himself into the police. A positive effect should cause a substantial improvement in the defendant's personal or social situation from the time of crime commitment.

The law enables the court when deciding on a sanction to consider such circumstances that can cause a penalty other than imprisonment. For example, if the act was a single case or if the accused has a problem with addiction and is in need of treatment.

For certain types of crimes, including perjury, the court will normally impose imprisonment. Crimes that have a high penal value are also usually punishable by imprisonment.

In connection with the issue of sanctions it can be mentioned that a crime can also involve other consequences for the accused, including

- Confiscation of property, i.e. the offender must give up certain property which he, for example, has used while committing the crime
- Expulsion from the country (only for foreigners)
- Compensation for damages, i.e. bodily injuries involving compensation for loss in income, burns, pain – both current and future.

- The driver's license will be withdrawn so that the accused will no longer have the right to drive a car. Such withdrawal is decided by the county administrative board and may be appealed to the general administrative court.

Checkpoint Chapter 5

Explain briefly what is meant by:

A.   Retaliation

B.   Talion principle

C.   Treatment Ideology

D.   Enlightenment

E.   Classical Criminal Law

F.   Crimes against a person

G.   Capital offence

H.   Crimes against public and state

I.   Violation of intellectual property laws

J.   Co-responsibility

K.   Conspiracy

L.   Terrorist offenses

M.   Sanction

N.   Conditional sentence

O.   Forfeiture

6

International Law

In universities the subject of international law has traditionally consisted of two subtopics: namely public international law and private international law (private and procedural international law). Using the term "international law" the focus has primarily been on public international law. Recently, international law and private international law have developed into two independent subjects at several universities in Sweden.

Private International Law

International private and procedural law is the area within the national legal system that regulates legal issues between countries. The rules mainly cover three issues:

- What country jurisdiction applies
- Law of what country should be administered (the choice of law)
- Whether a decision made in one country can be enforced in another country (recognition and enforcement).

An example of a matter in which private international law's provisions can be concerned is a dispute where the parties are in a contractual relationship, such as a purchase agreement, are residents of different countries and therefore the agreement will be covered by two legal systems. Another example can be environmental damage of sea pollution, which can affect sea fishing in several countries. Even in family law there are public international law provisions, for example, when spouses change homeland. In such a situation questions on the applicable laws for divorce, division of property, inheritance and wills can be brought to the fore in the new homeland.

The private international provisions normally concern the domestic law, but in some cases are related to international law (public international law) through international conventions or EU regulations.

Example

The International Sale of Goods Act (1987:822) is based on a UN convention and governs purchases between companies in different countries and begins as follows

§ 1, Articles 1-13 and 25-88 of the original texts of the United Nations Convention of 11 April 1980 on Contracts for International Sale of Goods shall be regarded as a law in this country. The original texts shall be equally valid.

Public International Law

Public international law is the legal system governing relations between the countries (states, nations). The public international law determined what rights and duties the states have towards each other. Besides states, public international law provisions to some extent concern international organizations and individuals, for example, human rights matters.

The main principle of public international law is that states are sovereign and legally equal to each other. Public international law, unlike domestic law, is a legal system where legal rules are created and implemented jointly by the states themselves. This is performed when states give their consent to be bound by a particular legal rule. Consent may be in written form (agreement, treaty, convention, arrangement, and protocol) or through practice (customary law). No state can be forced to enter into an agreement against their will. States are bound by rules that are generally regarded as customary law.

Examples of questions that may arise and that relate to public international law, according to the Department of Law at Stockholm University:

-   How are new legal rules in public international law established?
-   How can states be bound by the rules of public international law?
-   When can a new geographic entity be recognized as a new and independent state?

- What is the connection between national and international law?

- What power does a state court of justice have to exercise within their own territory?

- Who enjoys immunity (protection) against a state's exercise of power?

- When can a state be held liable for an act or omission?

- What opportunities do other countries have to control and influence the way a country treats its own citizens?

- When and how is it legal to use armed force in the international context?

- What rights and obligations does a state have with regard to the World Ocean and space?

- What international rules are used for the protection of the environment?

- How can the individuals responsible for serious violations of public international law be brought to justice?

The European Convention on Human Rights

An important part of public international law is how countries treat their citizens, i.e. what rights people have vs. the state. Human rights are protected by public international law, including conventions adopted by the UN and European Human Rights Council ("The Council of Europe"). The Council of Europe was founded in 1949 as a result of the atrocities committed in Europe and in the world during World War II. One of the organization's aims was to unite Europe and to create a document on human rights. A condition for a country to be a member of the Council of Europe is the respect for human rights. Today (2010) the Council of Europe consists of 47 European countries, the only exception is Belarus. The Council of Europe has no direct link to the EU, except for the fact that all the 27 EU countries are also members of the Council of Europe.

Secretary General of the Council of Europe, Thorbjörn Jagland, Norway

Thorbjörn Jagland, Norway, was elected as the new Secretary General of the Council of Europe on September 29, 2009.

The Council of Europe performs regular monitoring of how states fulfill the European Convention on Human Rights, as well as other European conventions in the legal, social and cultural spheres. The countries' observance is monitored partially through a reporting system and partially by a complaints mechanism which some organizations in the social sphere have the right to use in order to take care of their members' interests.

The Council of Europe in Strasbourg. Photo: Maria Jontén

Examples of rights in the Convention and its additional protocols are the prohibition of tortures, right to liberty and personal security, right to fair trial, right to the respect for private and family life, freedom of thought, conscience and religion, freedom of association and the right of assembly, prohibition of discrimination. Within the framework of the Council of Europe there have been adopted conventions on migration, refugees, extradition, terrorism and torture and other inhuman or degrading treatment or punishment. All member states of the Council of Europe are connected to the European convention, but not all have joined all the additional protocols which have been prepared later and which include additional rights.

Since 1995 the European Convention is a Swedish law, the Act (1994:1219) on the European Convention for the Protection of Human Rights and Basic Freedoms. Government Bill 1993/94: 117th includes a review of Swedish law's relation to the convention and how it is applied to complaints against Sweden.

In addition to the Convention on Human Rights, in 1961 the Council of Europe adopted a European Social Charter, revised in 1996, that included participation in labor market policies, working conditions, employment, freedom of association, right to negotiate, social security, family policy, etc.

The Council of Europe has a commissary for human rights that works to raise awareness of and respect for human rights in the member states. The commissary's tasks include pointing out of possible weaknesses in the laws, rules and practices that undermine the general objective of promoting respect for human rights in the Council of Europe's all the member countries. The European Court can hear complaints of individuals, private organizations or groups of individuals who feel that their rights and freedoms under the Convention or any of the additional protocols have been violated.

The European Court

The Council of Europe performs a judicial monitoring with the help of the European Court of Human Rights (the European Court) and the political monitoring of execution of the Court's judgments. Since its creation the European Court has announced more than 10,000 judgments. In addition a very large number of cases of complaints have been settled by the decision of the Court. States' obligations to fulfill their commitments under the Convention can be examined by an independent court, the European Court of Human Rights (the European Court). The European Court's decisions are legally binding on the states concerned.

The European Court can hear complaints of individuals, private organizations or groups of individuals who feel that their rights and freedoms under the Convention or any of the additional protocols have been violated. The first condition is that the state concerned is a member of the Convention and of the relevant additional protocol. Sweden has joined the Convention and the majority of the additional protocols.

A complaint must relate to a violation that has affected the complainant personally, and the violation must concern a right indicated in the Convention or in one of the additional protocols. A complaint cannot be directed against an individual or organization, but must be directed against a state and it must be an issue for which the State can be held responsible. It is not required to be a citizen of the state being complained of.

Anyone who wants to complain to the European Court must first seek adjudication in their own country by taking advantage of the opportunities available to challenge the authorities' and courts' decisions. In most cases it means that a complainant should take his case all the way to the highest instance in the country, such as the Supreme Court or the Supreme Administrative Court or to the government, depending on the nature of the case.

A complaint is received by the European Court within six months from the date when the final decision was reported by the state. Anonymous complaints are not admissible for examination, nor are any complaints that have already been examined by the court or by any other international body, such as any of the UN committees dealing with human rights.

The European Court

Liv Tigerstedt works as a legal official at the European Court.
Photo: Maria Jontén

Legal (Judicial) Work for the European Court Creates New Perspectives

Work, travel and discover the world. There are many possibilities when you have a degree in law, says Liv Tigerstedt and tells about exciting and diverse international work. She works as a legal officer at the European Court in Strasbourg - the European Court of Human Rights.

Since getting her degree in law at Lund more that ten years ago, Liv has lived and worked in countries like South Korea, Belarus and most recently she had a job with the UN Terrorism Committee in New York before returning to Strasbourg and her regular work at the European Court. The European Convention (ECHR) functions in Sweden as a law, and applies in all the Council of Europe member states.

Approximately 400 cases of a various nature are reported from Sweden each year to the department where Liv is working, and the number of cases tends to increase every year. Liv is dealing only with issues received from Sweden. One of the requirements for the Court to deal with a case is that it involves people or companies or other organizations that consider themselves personally mistreated by the authorities and courts in Sweden, and the cases that have already been tried in the highest instance (the Supreme Administrative Court or the

Supreme Court). The application must also fall within the competence area where someone's rights have been violated. This can include violent apprehension of children, convicted criminals who believe that there was a mistake in the criminal proceedings or matters that required an extremely long processing period by a Swedish authority.

Liv Tigerstedt explains that - The global situation significantly impacts the type of cases received, and that in recent years there have been many complaints regarding expulsions of people who have been refused a residence permit in Sweden. Liv Tigerstedt reviews the applications and discusses with the judges whether a case is appropriate for further investigation. This could result in a complaint not being passed for examination by the court. The European Court is therefore not an appeal instance; only approximately ten percent of the submitted cases from Sweden meet the formal requirements and are considered as well founded. Strong grounds are required for a case to be considered. If human rights have been violated in a Swedish court, the records are obtained from the Swedish government and authorities concerned. The administrative offices study whether there may be information on violation of the European Convention on Human Rights. The parties involved in the case will then get an opportunity to be heard in the proceedings. If the plaintiff succeeds in the European Court it does not mean that the verdict by the national court is changed. However, the plaintiff can receive compensation from the state for violation of his rights.

A large part of Liv Tigerstedt's work is the comparison of recently received cases with the cases received earlier. Depending on the previous results of the cases, she provides suggestions to the judge on the verdicts. The work can be similar to the work that a legal officer fulfills in the Swedish courts. The processing time of a case is normally about one to two years. The verdicts and the proposals are written in English or French, but it's also possible to send an applicaton in Swedish.

- The cases are determined by one, three, seven, or in rare cases seventeen judges. The Council of Europe appoints a judge from each member state, and currently there are 47 judges that are all elected for a period of nine years. The Swedish judge always considers cases that are received from Sweden. Sometimes the judges are in disagreement, however, in the European Court the majority decides. Only a few percent of cases lead to the observation of the judgment from the Swedish court. The European Court's decisions are legally binding on the State concerned.

- The idea is to alert the national courts on any problems so that they can fix them and follow the convention. We who work in the court are directly employed by the Council of Europe and have no real connection with the Swedish government. Before one is hired he has to pass a job interview as well as both written and oral tests. More than 650 people work at the European Court of which more than half are legal officers. We receive groups of visitors and we can show around people who are interested, who enjoy the international environment, says Liv Tigerstedt.

The European Court's Judgments

Decisions made by the European Court are legally binding on the state concerned. In the judgment the Court decides whether the state has violated the Convention or not. The court is, however, not the highest instance for national courts and authorities. It cannot change or obviate a decision made by a national authority or court, but may be guiding for future judgments.

The National Courts Administration (www.dom.se) publishes a newsletter on the European Convention for the Protection of Human Rights. The newsletter comes out eleven times a year in an electronic form. The purpose of the newsletter is to provide information on new decisions made by the European Court. In addition, it reports the cases settled in the Swedish courts in which the European Court has been mentioned.

Example

Huseyn and others against Azerbaijan, 2011-07-26

Several procedural rights under Article 6 were not met during the trial of four of the Azerbaijan opposition leaders charged with sedition in connection with the demonstrations which followed the opposition's loss in the presidential election. A violation of the right to a fair trial under Article 6.1 in conjunction with Article 6.3 b), c) and d) was obtained due appellants' counsel not receiving sufficient time for preparation, that the complainants were denied the right to defend themselves, that the right to effective defense had failed and that the court failed in its evaluation of evidence and justification as set forth in the testimony. Furthermore, there was a violation of the presumption of innocence under Article 6.2 due to statements of government officials during the legal process.

Source: News from the European Court 8/11, Swedish courts

Sigma Radio Television Ltd v Cyprus, 2011-07-21

The Cyprus Review Authority for Television and Radio fined television and radio broadcasters for multiple violations. One of the violations concerned the removal of racist and discriminatory observations in a television series. The European Court found that the Agency's assessments were within the framework margin to be assessed under Article 10 of what constitutes necessary restrictions on freedom of expression. Fines were also proportionate. There were therefore no violations of Article 10.

Source: News from the European Court 8/11, Swedish courts

United Nations

United Nations (UN) is the most important global organization with regard to human rights. After World War II there was a general feeling among the countries that founded the United Nations that the international community must share responsibility for individuals' fundamental rights.

In 1948 the UN General Assembly adopted the Universal Declaration of Human Rights. It is an international document that defines that all people have equal dignities and rights. The 30 Articles of the Universal Declaration of Human Rights have developed into a series of declarations and conventions.

The UN has also developed a system to facilitate and monitor observation of the regulations. There are special committees that correspond to the eight major conventions that meet annually to review compliance with the rules. In 2006 the UN Council on Human Rights was established which defines standards for human rights.

Extract the UN Universal Declaration of Human Rights.

- - - - - - - - - - - -

Article 1

All human beings are born free and equal in dignity and rights. They are endowed with reason and conscience and should act towards one another in a spirit of brotherhood.

Article 2

Everyone is entitled to all the rights and freedoms set forth in this Declaration, without distinction of any kind, such as race, colour, sex, language, religion, political or other opinion, national or social origin, property, birth or other status. Furthermore, no distinction shall be made on the basis of the political, jurisdictional or international status of the country or territory to which a person belongs, whether it be independent, trust, non–self–governing or under any other limitation of sovereignty.

Article 3

Everyone has the right to life, liberty and security of person.

Article 4

No one shall be held in slavery or servitude; slavery and the slave trade shall be prohibited in all their forms.

Article 5

No one shall be subjected to torture or to cruel, inhuman or degrading treatment or punishment.

Article 6

Everyone has the right to recognition everywhere as a person before the law.

Article 7

All are equal before the law and are entitled without any discrimination to equal protection of the law. All are entitled to equal protection against any discrimination in violation of this Declaration and against any incitement to such discrimination.

- - - - - - - - - - - - -

The Universal Declaration is a norm, not a law. Many pacts, conventions and treaties that contain the main elements of the Declaration of 1948 are signed and are in force, and most member countries have ratified (accepted) them. What determines the Convention's role is the number of countries that ratify it. The countries that ratify the Convention oblige themselves to follow it. Some conventions state that the UN has the right to check if governments follow the conventions and protect citizens' rights and fundamental freedoms in accordance with what is stipulated in the conventions. In Sweden, the conventions have been included in Swedish legislation as the Act on the European Convention on Protection for Human Rights and Fundamental Freedoms (1994:1219).

A so-called Commissioner for Human Rights was established by the UN General Assembly in 1993. The Commissioner's role is to promote and protect human rights through dialogue and advice to UN member countries, including through the coordination of activities within the UN system of human rights.

UN High Commissioner for Refugees' (UNHCR) task is to assist refugees and to protect their rights. There are UNHCR agencies in about 120 countries. UNHCR's efforts to protect refugees are based on the UN Refugee Convention and on the additional protocol of 1967 which expanded the applicability of the 1951 Convention.

UN Convention on the Rights of the Child

A child is, according to the Convention, every person under 18 years, unless the child comes of age earlier under the law of the child's home country. The Convention includes civil, political, economic, social and cultural rights. The UN Convention on the Rights of the Child has four basic principles that should guide the interpretation of the Convention's other articles:

- Prohibition of discrimination (Article 2)
- The best interests of the child should be the main concern (Article 3)
- The right to life and development (Article 6)
- The right to be heard (Article 12)

These basic principles also mean that every child, without exception, has right

- to get information on their rights,
- for the child's best interests to be considered in all decisions affecting the child;
- for not just the child's survival, but also his or her development to be ensured to the maximum capacity of society
- for the child's views to come forward and be shown respect.

The fundamental principles all together form an attitude towards children that could be called the Convention's view of children. The Convention's principles have been incorporated into Swedish law, the Children and Parents Code (1949:381)

The Humanitarian Law

All armed conflicts and wars should be prevented, and that is why it is forbidden to start war under the UN Charter. But if war does occur, the harmful effects must be limited. International humanitarian law, also called the laws of war, is the system of rules that states have agreed upon in order to protect people and reduce human sufferings in the result of war. The purpose of humanitarian law is to protect people not taking part in the war and also provide certain protection for the combatants.

Humanitarian law consists of two parts:

- Rules that protect those who are not participating in hostilities, such as civilians, wounded and sick combatants and prisoners of war. These categories of people may not be attacked, but should be protected and respected.

- Rules that protect those who fight, so-called combatants. These rules are intended to protect the combatants from unnecessary suffering and injuries by limiting the types of weapons and methods of warfare that may be used.

The humanitarian law cannot directly prevent an armed conflict. However, if the humanitarian law is respected during the war, it is possible to reduce the effects of war and make peace possible when the war is over. It is therefore important to disseminate information about and teach international humanitarian law before an armed conflict breaks out, e.g. by the UN, Red Cross and others.

The humanitarian law in connection with armed conflicts is governed by the four Geneva Conventions which were developed in 1949. A basic principle of the Conventions is that civilians and even injured, sick or captured soldiers should be protected. Refugees are protected by the Refugee Convention of 1951.

International crime

There are three main international crimes in the public international law: genocide, crimes against humanity and violations of humanitarian law by war crimes. According to the public international law Sweden has the opportunity to apply the so-called universal jurisdiction to international crimes. This means that the Swedish judicial system has the opportunity to investigate such crimes and prosecute suspects in trials in Sweden regardless of who committed such crimes and where.

Such a responsibility of bringing the perpetrators to justice can be applied only in the case of violations of the Geneva Conventions in international conflicts (the laws of war) and in case of genocide committed on Swedish territory.

International Courts and Tribunals

The international courts play an important role in public international law enforcement, both for prevention and stopping of violations of international law. Above all there are two types of trials in the international system.

Settlement of Disputes between States

The first type's aim is to contribute to peaceful settlement of disputes between states. Here belong such types of courts as the United Nations' International Court of Justice and the Permanent Court of Arbitration, both are located in The Hague, Netherlands. The International Court of Justice was founded in 1945 while the Permanent Court of Arbitration has functioned since 1899.

Case Example

2010/10 - The Court finds that Uruguay has breached its procedural obligations to co-operate with Argentina and the Administrative Commission of the River Uruguay (CARU) during the development of plans for the CMB (ENCE) and Orion (Botnia) pulp mills - The Court declares that Uruguay has not breached its substantive obligations for the protection of the environment provided for by the Statute of the River Uruguay by authorizing the construction and commissioning of the Orion (Botnia) mill.

Bringing People to Justice

The second type of international courts' aim is to bring individuals to justice for gross crimes against the international law. These courts began to be established in the 1990s. They can both be temporary and be created for a special situation, such as the International Criminal Tribunal for the Former Yugoslavia and the International Criminal Tribunal for Rwanda, and permanent, such as the International Criminal Court, ICC.

International Criminal Court

On the 1st of July 2002, the Rome Statute of the International Criminal Court went into effect. Sweden and the EU have always supported establishment of the ICC which is considered as an important part of the public international law and represents an important step towards the punishment of gross crimes against the so-called humanitarian law. The court is located in The Hague in the Netherlands, and its inauguration and swearing-in of 18 judges took place in March 2003.

The court has a right (mandate) to adjudicate crimes of genocide, crimes against humanity and war crimes. The mandate applies only to offenses committed after the Rome Statute came legally in force on 1 July 2002. The court may bring a person to justice in the following five cases.

-   If the act has taken place in a state that is a party to the Rome Statute.
-   If the act has taken place in a state that submitted a certain declaration that the state had accepted the court's jurisdiction.
-   If the person accused of the crime is a resident of a country that is a party to the Rome Statute.
-   If the person accused is a resident of a country that has submitted a certain declaration that the state had accepted the court's jurisdiction.
-   If the UN Security Council submitted a case to the court.

The court can deal with suspected crimes in three different ways: a member state can submit a case to the court when suspicions of a crime have occurred; similarly, the UN Security Council submits suspected crimes to the court; a prosecutor at the court can initiate an investigation on his own initiative.

The ICC is complementary to national courts and starts working on a case when national courts fail to fulfill their duty. If the crime is investigated or has been investigated by a state that wishes and has the opportunity to investigate and prosecute the crime, the ICC cannot intervene. The principal task of the court is to prevent possible impunity that may arise with regard to this type of crime. This is done primarily by encouraging the countries to investigate and prosecute crimes on their own, and secondly by providing an international body in the form of the ICC.

International Criminal Tribunal for the Former Yugoslavia (ICTY)

The disintegration of Yugoslavia in the early 1990s gave rise to widespread war among the new states in the Balkans. Serious crimes were committed during the wars in the form of mass executions, dispossessions of people, tortures and rapes. This led to strong reactions around the world and the result was an international tribunal where the guilty people could be brought to justice.

On May 25, 1993, the UN Security Council founded a temporary tribunal for prosecution of people responsible for serious violations of public international law committed in the former Yugoslavia after 1990. The name of the tribunal was the International Criminal Tribunal for the former Yugoslavia, ICTY. The Tribunal is located in The Hague, Netherlands, and adjudicates four types of crimes: gross violations of the 1949 Geneva Conventions, violations of the laws of war or common law, genocide and crimes against humanity.

The Security Council's decisions are binding on all UN member states and are obliged to cooperate with the Tribunal to ensure that the authorities execute its requests. The establishment of the ICTY was an historical event, it was the first time when the Council created an international tribunal for international peace and security and the first international tribunal for war crimes since the Nuremberg and Tokyo Tribunals after World War II.

All investigations were supposed to be completed by 2004, all trials in the first instance to be completed in 2008, and all the work was done in 2010. http://www.icty.org

International Criminal Tribunal for Rwanda

The International Criminal Tribunal for Rwanda, ICTR, was established by resolution of the UN Security Council. The Court's mission is to prosecute and adjudicate people responsible for gross violations of international humanitarian law committed during the genocide in Rwanda in 1994. UN member states are obliged to cooperate with the tribunal and to ensure that the countries' authorities execute their requests.

On April 6, 1994, Rwanda's ex-president who belonged to the majority Hutu group was murdered. Within a couple of hours genocide in which both Tutsis and Hutus took part began. Obviously, the murder had been carefully planned in advance. When the genocide groups, so-called militias, in mid-July 1994 suffered a military defeat of the civil war, about 800,000 people had been murdered.

The International Criminal Tribunal for Rwanda implemented adjudications of three types of crimes: genocide, crimes against humanity and violations of Common Article 3 of the 1949 Geneva Conventions. The tribunal's headquarters are in Arusha, Tanzania.

All investigations were to be completed in 2004, all trials in the first instance were to be completed in 2008 and all work was supposed to be done in 2010.

The Special Court for Sierra Leone

The Special Court for Sierra Leone was established in 2002 by an agreement between the UN and the government of Sierra Leone. The court's aim was to try people responsible for violations of humanitarian law as well as for breach of certain national laws committed in Sierra Leone since 30 November 1996.

The background is the civil war that started in 1991 when the rebel movement known as the Revolutionary United Front (RUF) was formed. The civil war lasted for ten years and cost 200,000 people their lives. The war was characterized by serious abuses such as forced use of child soldiers, mutilations and rapes.

The Special Court is the first court that is a mixture of international and national courts created to try violations of international humanitarian law. Unlike the Tribunals for Rwanda (ICTR) and the former Yugoslavia (ICTY), the Special Court for Sierra Leone has prosecutors and judges both from the country where the crimes were committed, appointed by the Government of Sierra Leone, and from other countries, appointed by UN Secretary General. The Special Court was located in Freetown, Sierra Leone, and was not expected to work for more than three years and is funded by voluntary contributions.

Lawsuits against the Khmer Rouge

During the Khmer Rouge's governing in the present day's Cambodia (then Kampuchea) between 1975 and 1979 the number of the population has been diminished by almost one-fifth partly due to executions, starvation and diseases. Millions of people were displaced and between one and two million people died. The exact number of casualties will never be defined. In 1998 the United Nations and Cambodia held negotiations on the establishment of a tribunal to try the crimes committed under the Khmer Rouge.

On May 13, 2003, the UN General Assembly decided upon a resolution on trials in Cambodia against the Khmer Rouge leaders. An agreement on how the trials will be executed was preceded by five years of negotiations between the UN Secretary-General and the Cambodian government. The negotiations were terminated one time by the Secretary General because of lack of commitment by the Cambodian government. Cambodia's parliament approved (ratified) the agreement in October 2004.

The trials against the Khmer Rouge are a national legal process with both national and international judges and prosecutors. They differ from the International Criminal Tribunals for the Former Yugoslavia (ICTY) and Rwanda (ICTR). Prosecutions took place against those of the Khmer Rouge who were responsible for the violations of Cambodian law and certain international laws in the former Kampuchea between 1975 and 1979.

Checkpoint Chapter 6

Explain briefly what is meant by:
A. International law
B. Public international law
C. The Council of Europe
D. Convention
E. Human rights
F. The European Court
G. United Nations

H. The International Court of Justice

I. The International Criminal Court

J. Tribunal

Appendix 1

Comparison of the legal systems in Sweden and in Belarus

(Based on a visit to Belarus in December 2011
by Cege Ekström and the lawyer Leif Östling in a project funded by
the Swedish Institute-SI)

- National legislation in Belarus consists of thirteen kinds of legal rules, including the president's decrees or directives. In addition there are five forms of regulation for local governments and government regulations. In Sweden we have only legislation through parliamentary decisions, regulations with detailed requirements and detailed regulations from authorities.

- The Belarusian Constitution includes the following articles on human rights:

"The basis of the Constitutional system, enshrined in Article 2 of the Constitution, is the principle of protection of human rights and freedom and the guarantees of their realization as the highest value and purpose of the functioning of the society and state"

Nevertheless Belarus is by international observers regarded as an undemocratic country, which is controlled by a person, the president Lukashenka. The population has, as it seems, limited human rights and freedoms. Belarus is the only European country that is not a member of the European Council and therefore has not adopted the European Convention on Human Rights into its legislation.

- The president of Belarus is the head of state with a lot more power than the Swedish head of state - the king.

- Belarus has military courts which do not exist in Sweden.

- As many former Soviet states, Belarus has a constitutional court directly under the government that determines whether the legislation and the application of laws is in accordance with the fundamental law (Constitution). In Sweden there is no equivalent to such a body, and these functions apply to several bodies, i.e. the Council on Legislation, the Chancellor of Justice, etc.

- The Belarusian courts are directly subordinated to the Ministry of Justice, i.e. the government. The courts of Sweden are independent from the government and have a separate authority responsible for administration, facilities, personnel, but cannot influence court judgments.

- The Swedish division between administrative courts and civil courts is not equivalent to that in Belarus. Belarusian district courts are responsible for administrative cases, criminal and civil cases between private individuals. Commercial courts adjudicate cases between businesses, and between companies and private individuals, and authorities with regard to economic issues.

- Verdicts of first instance can be appealed to a court of appeal which can be located in the same building and even have the same personnel. In Sweden, the first and second instance courts are separate bodies.

- In Belarus, as in many Southern European countries, there are notaries who approve and register real property purchase contracts, apartment purchases, wills and estate inventories. The handling is based mainly on written documents that are not included in databases.

- Belarusian police departments, city police, traffic police, and police officers belong to the Ministry of Internal Affairs that reports directly to the Ministry of Justice. In Sweden there is the National Police agency which is a body separate from the local police authorities and separate from the government.

- The Belarusian police special forces use military-style uniforms and military-style vehicles, which is not possible in Sweden where people should clearly distinguish between the police and the military.

- The Belarusian security police, the KGB (Committee for State Security), is separate from the Ministry of Internal Affairs and works on its own. The Swedish Security Service is a police service that deals with regular police activities.

Other comments:

Our impression is that the Belarusian legal system seems, on the surface, to function surprisingly well considering that it was built during the 20 years after Belarus had left the Soviet Union. These features provide a credible and modern impression and the trials we attended were held in a seemingly correct way, except for certain differences from the Swedish practice. Even when we had meetings with judges they gave a serious and credible impression as well as did the police. The number of cases has increased dramatically, mainly civil cases, which according to the judges is due to the increased confidence among the public.

Of course, we have no evidence that the application is made in an impartial manner. We can also note that the courts do not have such an independence from political power as they do in Sweden and the presidential power seems to be strong in the legislation (see above). During our visit to Belarus (week 49 2011), we could monitor the ongoing situation and observed the so called terrorist trial in Minsk in the mass media. Our personal impression was that it was not held in a correct way from a Swedish or European viewpoint, which was also strengthened by the comments of the independent Belarusian Internet mass media.

However, we believe that increased knowledge and experience exchanged at the operational court level would strengthen the relatively new Belarusian legal system and, in perspective, the Belarusian democracy. One possibility would be to invite Belarusian judges to seminars in Sweden together with judges and representatives of the Swedish legal system.

Appendix 2

Foundations of the Constitutional System of the Republic of Belarus

Author: Zhanna Kanavalava

The basis of the constitutional system, enshrined in Article 2 of the Constitution, is the principle of protection of human rights and freedom and the guarantees of their realization as the highest value and purpose of the functioning of the society and state. Article 3 of the Constitution states that the state and national sovereignty are also the bases of the constitutional system. The people are the only source of state power and the bearer of sovereignty in the Republic of Belarus. Article 6 of the Constitution establishes that state power is exercised on the basis of its division into legislative, executive and judicial branches. The principle of checks and balances requires cooperation between these separate and independent state bodies. The rule of law is set forth in Article 7 of the Constitution. The state and all its authorities and officials are required to act within the scope of the Constitution and the laws enacted in accordance with its legislative acts.

Legislative power in the Belarusian state is represented by the Parliament known as the National Assembly of the Republic of Belarus. This is the only state agency that considers, approves or declines draft legislation (proposed law). Parliament in its structure consists of two chambers - the House of Representatives and the Council of the Republic. The House of Representatives considers draft legislation whereas the Council of the Republic approves or declines it.

The President of the Republic of Belarus is the head of state and the guarantor of the Constitution of the Republic of Belarus, human and citizen rights and freedoms. The Head of State has the right granted by law to accept decrees, having the force of law, as well as the edicts and orders.

The Government of the Republic of Belarus - Council of Ministers is the central body of state administration. The Government reports and is accountable to the President of the Republic of Belarus in its activity, and is answerable to the Parliament of the Republic of Belarus. In its structure, the Government of the Republic of Belarus consists of the Prime Minister, his deputies and ministers.

The judicial power, exercised independently of the legislative and executive branches of government, belongs to the courts and will be considered separately in this paper.

The bodies of state control and supervision have been created and operate in accordance with the Constitution. The Prosecutor's Office and the State Control Committee belong to these bodies according to the Constitution of the Republic of Belarus. The territory of Belarus is divided into administrative units that are managed by local governments and authorities, which include local councils, as well as the local executive of the Committee and administration areas in the city.

The main sources of law in Belarus

The main sources of law in Belarus are the regulations, and the regulations are:

The Constitution of the Republic of Belarus - the Fundamental Law of the Republic of Belarus, having supreme legal force and enshrines fundamental principles and norms of the legal regulation of the major public-safety relationships;

Decision of the referendum - legislative act aimed at settlement of important issues of public life, adopted by national or local referendum.

Programmatic law - law adopted in accordance with the Constitution of the Republic of Belarus and the procedure for certain issues that have been identified by the Constitution.

Code - law, which provides complete system regulation of a certain area of society (e.g., Civil Code). There are 40 codes (in the Russian text it is 40, but my research also shows that there are 27 codes) in Belarus. The codes are created to organize and streamline the law;

Law - legal acts which establish the principles and regulations of the most important societal relations.

Presidential Decree - legal acts of the Head of State, which have the force of law, issued in accordance with the Constitution of the Republic of Belarus;

Presidential Edict - normative legal act of the President, published in order to implement his power;

Directive of the President of the Republic of Belarus - programmatic edict, issued by the Head of State for the systemic issues that have significant political, social and economic importance;

Resolution of the Parliament - National Assembly of the Republic of Belarus;

Resolution of the Council of Ministers - are the most important by-law acts as published on governance of the country's economy, providing the state policy in the spheres of science, education, social welfare, public-order, etc.;

Acts of the Constitutional Court, Supreme Court of the Republic of Belarus (Resolutions of the Plenum of the Supreme Court of the Republic of Belarus), the Supreme Economic Court of the Republic of Belarus (Resolutions of the Plenum of the Supreme Economic Court of Belarus), and the Attorney General of the Republic of Belarus;

Resolutions of ministries, state committees and the National Bank of Belarus (the National Bank of the Republic of Belarus, the Board of Directors of the National Bank of Belarus) - acts taken collectively on the basis and in pursuance of legal acts of greater legal force within the competence of the relevant public authorities. This is the largest group of by-law acts, regulating societal relations on more narrow specific issues.

Regulations - Acts adopted (issued) by the Head of State, the legislative, executive, judiciary and local government and self-containing set of rules governing the procedure of the relevant authorities;

Direction - an act defining the detailed content and methodological issues of regulation in a specific area of society;

Rules - codified legal acts, that specify general rules for the purpose of regulating the behavior of the subjects of societal relations in certain areas and on procedural matters;

Statute (regulations) - acts that specify the procedure of statement authority (organization), and the regulation of civil servants and other persons in certain areas;

Order – the act, issued by the head of the republican body of state authority within the jurisdiction of the primary authority in the relevant field of public administration;

Decisions of the Local Government - normative legal acts adopted by the local Council of Deputies, by the Executive and administrative authorities within their competence to deal with local issues and are binding on the respective territory.

National Register of Legal Acts of the Republic of Belarus - accounting system of legal acts that make up the laws of the Republic of Belarus.

Legal acts included in the National Register are placed in the master database of legal information, as well as published in the official periodical "National Register of the Republic of Belarus" (frequency of publication - 12 issues per month), and its electronic version with the registration number of the National Register.

Maintaining the National Register of Legal Acts of the Republic of Belarus on paper and in electronic form, as well as the official publication of the periodical "The National Register of the Republic of Belarus" is carried out by **the National Center of Legal Information of the Republic of Belarus**.

Law enforcement system of the republic of Belarus

The judicial system is the set of all active courts in the Republic of Belarus, established by the Constitution of the Republic of Belarus, Code of the Republic of Belarus on judicial system and status of judges, and other legal acts.

According to Article 5 of the Code of the Republic of Belarus on judicial system and status of judges, the judicial system of the Republic of Belarus shall include the following elements:

1) **Constitutional Justice**: The Constitutional Court of the Republic of Belarus. The Constitutional Court has the objectives of securing the supremacy of the Constitution and its direct application on the territory of the state by reviewing **new legislation and statutes** to assure that they are drafted in accordance with the Constitution, by resolving contradictions of normative legal acts of state and local bodies to the Constitution, and by otherwise strengthening legality in rule-making and the enforcement of law.

2) **Courts of general jurisdiction**: General courts include the Supreme Court of the Republic of Belarus, regional (Minsk city) courts, district (city) and military courts.

    Regional Courts and the Minsk City Court form the second level of the Belarusian court system, and bridge the hierarchy between the district (city) courts and the Supreme Court of the Republic of Belarus.

    Courts of second instance consider civil and criminal cases within its jurisdiction as a Court of First Instance, by way of supervision and on newly discovered evidence, as well as supervision of cases on administrative violations. These courts may, in accordance with the laws within its jurisdiction, consider civil and criminal cases on appeal.

    Military courts, in contrast to the general court, are not organized with respect to administrative-territorial division of the country, and are on a territorial basis by geographical location and given the number of units of the Armed Forces of the Republic of Belarus. Military courts administer justice for individuals of military status, The Supreme Court of the Republic of Belarus is the highest court in the system of courts of general jurisdiction. The Supreme Court hears cases in the order of supervision and on newly discovered evidence, as court of appeal, as well as a court of first instance - the most complex criminal and civil cases.

3) **The economic courts**: the Supreme Economic Court of the Republic of Belarus, and the Economic courts of the regions (Minsk city).

    The economic courts of the Republic of Belarus shall administer justice by resolving economic (economic) disputes arising from civil, administrative, land, financial and other public interaction, including the participation of international organizations, foreign individuals and citizens.

In Belarus, there are also the International Court of Arbitration (established April 12, 1994 at Belarusian Chamber of Commerce and Industry of the fallen, those) and the CIS Economic Court.

4) **The judges:** Judges have specific qualification requirements, including specific requirements for candidates for posts as judges, the order of appointment, tenure and termination of powers.

Judge of the Constitutional Court may be appointed (elected) a citizen of the Republic of Belarus, who is proficient in the Belarusian and Russian languages, has a higher legal education, is a highly qualified expert in the field of law who as a rule possess a scientific degree and high moral qualities.

Candidate for judge of a general or economic court shall be a citizen of the Republic of Belarus who has reached the age of 25, who is proficient in the Belarusian and Russian languages, has a higher legal education with qualification "lawyer" experience in the specialty for at least three years, has not committed discrediting actions, and has passed a qualifying exam for the post of judge.

A candidate for a position of judge of the regional courts (Minsk City) and the Belarusian military courts should have at least three years' work experience as a judge ; and an applicant for a position of judge of the Supreme Court, except for the judges of the judicial panelof the intellectual property cases of the Supreme Court and the Supreme Economic Court of Belarus - at leastfive years' experience.

The following people cannot be appointed as judges:

1) The person against whom there is entered into force a guilty verdict of the court;

2) A person incapable for health reasons to serve as a judge, as confirmed by medical opinion;

3)   The person declared incapable or incompetent by a court, which entered into force.

Citizens of the Republic of Belarus have the right to participate in the court of justice as lay judges in the manner and cases stipulated by legislative acts of the Republic of Belarus. The peer reviews of criminal cases are implemented by the court consisting of a judge and two assessors.

In accordance with Article 133 of the Code of the Republic of Belarus on judicial system and status of judges, assessors may be nationals of the Republic of Belarus who have reached the age of 25 years, proficient in the Belarusian and Russian languages.

It's impossible to be an assessor if:

- The person against whom a court verdict is entered;
- A person found incapable or incompetent in the manner prescribed by law;
- Persons who are registered in the Substance Abuse and neuropsychiatric dispensaries;
- The House of Representatives, members of the National Assembly of the Republic of Belarus, the executives of national government bodies and other government officials whose positions are included in the personnel register of the Head of State of the Republic of Belarus, judges, prosecutors, court staff, institutions of justice, law enforcement officers, financial investigations and national security, notaries, lawyers, and persons occupying elective positions in local government and self-government;
- The clergy.

The National Council of Judges is the judicial autonomous body. The qualifying judicial panels are organized on the basis of eligibility, interchangeability (alternativeness) and accountability to the bodies that elected them. Accountability of the qualifying judicial panels does not apply to the adoption of decisions (conclusions) on specific issues.

The supreme body of self-government judges is *the Congress of Judges of the Republic of Belarus*, which meets once every four years.

The Bar in the Republic of Belarus is an independent legal institution designed in accordance with the Constitution to provide professional advocacy work.

Any natural or legal person in the Republic of Belarus may apply for legal aid to a lawyer (by choice) to protect the rights and legitimate interests in the courts, other agencies and organizations.

The Bar is not included in the state apparatus, is not a public authority or local authority, and has no right to state coercion of persons who have committed a violation of the law. Actions and decisions of the legal profession are not of a universally binding character.

Activities of lawyers:

- Provide advice and clarification on the legal issues, both oral and written information on the legislation;
- Draft account statements, complaints and other documents of a legal nature;
- Work in courts and other bodies and organizations in civil cases and administrative cases;
- Participate in the preliminary investigation and court proceedings in criminal cases of the quality of the defenders, as well as representatives of the victims, civil plaintiffs, and civil defendants;
- Provide persons and legal entities with legal assistance.

Legal assistance provided by lawyers, as a rule, is paid.

Assistance is provided free of charge by bar associations at their own expense to the plaintiffs in the trial courts in the conduct of cases involving employment, alimony, compensation for damage caused by injury or other impairment of health-related work, as well as disabled people of 1 and 2 groups of disability during consultations that do not require familiarization with the case, during consultations on matters notrelated to entrepreneurial activities, the Great Patriotic War participants, the servicemen and citizens under the age of 18.

A Lawyer of the Republic of Belarus is required to be:

1) a citizen of the Republic of Belarus, 2) have a higher legal education, 3) experience in the profession for at least three years, and 4) or not having such experience, but was observing and training for a period of six months to one year at the Bar, 5) who has passed a qualifying examination, 6) has received a license to practice as an advocate.

Notariat of the Republic of Belarus shall include the public and private notaries, authorized officials and diplomatic agents of diplomatic missions of the Republic of Belarus and consular officers of consular establishments of the Republic of Belarus, to protect the rights and lawful interests of citizens and legal entities, the public interest by notarial act on behalf of the Republic of Belarus.

Notarial acts are carried out in public notarial offices, which are formed by the Ministry of Justice of the Republic of Belarus in the regions, cities and districts in the cities.

In Minsk and cities that are regional centers, one of the public notaries established as the first public notary's office, which can be imposed commission the most difficult notary acts.

Public notary offices are not legal if particles and are under the Ministry of Justice of the Republic of Belarus.

Requirements for the person claiming to occupy the post of Notary Public:

- Citizenship of the Republic of Belarus;
- The presence of higher legal education;
- A certificate on the right to engage in notarial activities;
- Compliance with other requirements of the legislation of the Republic of Belarus.

Ministry of Justice is the central body of executive power in the Republic of Belarus, ensuring the implementation of state policy in the sphere of justice.

The system of the Ministry of Justice of the Republic of Belarus includes the Department of Justice regional and Minsk city executive committees, public notaries, Scientific Research Institute for Criminology, Criminalistics and Forensic Sciences and the National Labor arbitration; registry office, the Unified state register of legal entities of the Ministry of Justice Belarus, legal research and practical journal "Justice Belarus.

Prosecutor's Office of the Republic of Belarus - a unified and centralized system of bodies exercising on behalf of the state supervision over the strict and uniform enforcement of laws, decrees and regulations in the Republic of Belarus, as well as performs other functions specified in legislation.

The Attorney General (Procurator-General) and subordinate prosecutors are charged with supervising the exact and uniform implementation of laws, decrees, orders and other regulations by ministries and other subordinate bodies of the Council of Ministers, the local representative and executive bodies, organizations and institutions, public associations, officials and citizens. Article 125 of the Constitution further states that "The Procurator's office shall exercise supervision over the implementation of the laws determining the execution of the verdicts of the courts in civil, criminal and administrative cases in instances determined by the law, as well as shall carry out preliminary investigation and support state charges in the courts."

The Attorney General is the head of the Prosecutor's office, is appointed by and is accountable to the President

The system of territorial prosecutor's offices of the Republic of Belarus has three levels:

1. Prosecutor General's office of the Republic of Belarus, which is the central body of the prosecution;

2. Prosecutor's office areas, Minsk;

3. Prosecutor's Office districts, districts in cities, towns, inter-district prosecutor overseeing the execution of the laws in several areas.

Among the specialized prosecutors are Belarusian transport prosecutor's office and subordinate downstream transport prosecutor's office, the Belarusian military prosecutor's office and subordinate military prosecutor's office. In addition, in the republic prosecutor's office is also involved with the supervision of enforcement of laws in correctional institutions.

An employee of the prosecutor's office should be a citizen of the Republic of Belarus, have a law degree, possess the necessary professional and moral qualities and meet other requirements of the legislation on public service.

Legal counselling department (of an organization).

A separate department – legal counselling department (bureau) – can be created in an organization, or a position of a leading (main) legal adviser, legal adviser or deputy head on legal issues, who is responsible for the legal counselling department's activities management.

Legal services can be rendered to an organization on a contractual basis by lawyers, legal entities or entrepreneurs who have a special permission (license) for such type of activities.

The legal counselling department is subordinated to the head of the organization.

Interior affairs agencies - state police, engaged in the fight against crime, providing public order and ensuring public safety in accordance with the tasks assigned to them by this Law and other legislative acts of the Republic of Belarus.

The Ministry of Interior Affairs is the governmental authority that heads the interior affairs bodies and interior troops, carrying within its powers to regulate and control the fight against crime, public order, public security and coordination in this area other republican bodies of state administration.

The system of interior affairs bodies shall include:

- Police - a system of units, designed to protect the life, health, honor, dignity, rights, freedoms and lawful interests of citizens whose rights and legitimate interests of organizations, the interests of society and the State from illegal encroachments.

The police consist of:

- **The criminal police** - solves the problem of prevention, detection, crime prevention, tracing the perpetrators, fugitives from the authorities conducting criminal process, persons avoiding punishment, missing persons and other persons in the cases stipulated by legislative acts of the Republic Belarus, the identification of unidentified corpses.

The structure of the criminal police division includes Criminal Investigation to combat economic crime, drug control and human trafficking, the fight against corruption and organized crime, forensic and other units.

- **The public security police** - operational-duty service, police services, criminal-executive inspection, inspection of juvenile police unit drill, the State Automobile Inspection, Road Patrol

Service, a unit designed to hold perpetrators of crimes and administrative offense, as well as other units.

- **Other units** that are created to perform police tasks and report to the Minister of the Interior.

- **Departments of the preliminary investigation** - Since 1 January 2012 the Investigative Committee of the Republic of Belarus was formed. Its main task is the comprehensive, complete, impartial and prompt investigation of crime. Investigative departments will be transferred to this committee.

- **Units on citizenship and migration** - are implementing measures aimed at implementing the legislation on citizenship and migration, including the exit and entry into the Republic of Belarus citizens of movement and choice of place of residence, the legal status of foreigners and stateless persons on refugee status or subsidiary or temporary protection or asylum in the Republic of Belarus;

- **Units of protection** - performing functions in the field of security management, protection of public order protected sites, in areas of posts and patrol routes.

- **Departments of Finance and logistics** - are organizing the financial and logistical activities of internal affairs and internal security forces, provide them with funding and centralized supply of material resources, develop and implement measures aimed at creating the necessary social conditions;

- **Authorities and institutions of the correctional system** - serve:

a) the execution and serving of punishment in the form of restriction of liberty, arrest, imprisonment, life imprisonment, execution of sentences of capital punishment, deprivation of the right to occupy certain positions or engage in certain activities designated as an additional punishment;

b) Compulsory isolation and medical-social rehabilitation with obligation to work of citizens who are in treatment-labor dispensaries;

c) The execution of preventive measures in the form of detention, acts of amnesty and pardon;

d)   Investigation of persons avoiding penal.

The general management of internal affairs authorities exercised by the President of the Republic of Belarus and the Council of Ministers within the authority delegated to him by the President of the Republic of Belarus.

The direct management of internal affairs bodies The Minister of Internal Affairs.

Crimes in the Criminal Code are divided into the following categories, depending on the degree of danger to society:

1)   Crimes that do not pose great danger to society (e.g., assaults);

2)   Less severe (e.g., failure to repay accounts payable);

3)   Severe (e.g., forced to commit the transaction or to refuse to commit to the use of violence against the victim);

4)   Very serious (murder under aggravating circumstances).

Also distinguish the crime:

-    Against the person (murder, causing grievous bodily harm, kidnapping),

-    Against property (theft, robbery, extortion, fraud),

-    Against the order of economic activities (smuggling, illegal business activities, consumer fraud),

-    Against the environmental safety and the environment (land damage, pollution, forest),

-    Against public safety and public health (terrorism, hostage-taking)

-    Against public order and public morality (hooliganism,-knows about the danger of a false report) and others.

Criminal liability for a crime begins at 16 years of age. However, for certain offenses (an exhaustive list of which is contained in the law such as for murder, rape and robbery), the age of criminal responsibility is reduced to 14 years.